TIMESAVER FOR EXAMS

Vocabulary

FOR FIRST (FCE)

By Helen Chilton

Contents

Introduction

Who is this book for?

This book is for teachers of students who are preparing for the *Cambridge English: First* or *Cambridge English: First for Schools* exam and who require extra practice material. Ideal as a supplement to any *Cambridge English: First* or upper-intermediate coursebook, the topics and activities are designed to appeal to older teenage and young adult classes. This resource is also suitable for use with any upper-intermediate classes who wish to develop their speaking skills and broaden their vocabulary at B2 level.

The *Cambridge English: First* exam – an overview

Cambridge English: First is a qualification at upper-intermediate level (level B2 on the CEFR scale) which is officially recognised by universities, employers and governments around the world. The exam is aimed at learners who want to use English for study at an upper-intermediate level, start working in an English-speaking environment or live independently in an English-speaking country.

The *Cambridge English: First for Schools* exam is a version of the *Cambridge English: First* exam which follows the same format and is at the same level. The *Cambridge English: First for Schools* exam contains content and topics which are especially appropriate for school-age learners.

How does this book help your exam students?

The *Cambridge English: First* exam requires students to have a wide-ranging vocabulary at B2 level. The activities in this book provide practice to help both broaden and deepen students' lexical knowledge across a range of skills and topics.

- In the Reading and Use of English test, students are required to demonstrate knowledge of idiom and fixed phrases, collocation, synonyms, word formation and text organisation as well as demonstrate good reading skills. The lessons in the Reading section focus on building students' receptive knowledge of a wide range of vocabulary. Some items may be familiar and need consolidation and some will be new.

- In the Writing test, a proportion of the marks is awarded specifically for range and accuracy of lexical resource. Students need to select vocabulary which is relevant to the topic and appropriate in style and register; appropriate use of less common lexis is also acknowledged. The activities in this Timesaver give plenty of opportunity for vocabulary development, enabling students to make appropriate and accurate choice of lexical item as well as demonstrate their breadth of knowledge.

- In the Speaking test, marks are awarded to students who are able to demonstrate a range of appropriate vocabulary to give and exchange views on a wide range of familiar topics. The activities in this section focus on key topic areas from the exam as well as offering strategies to help students make the most of their language in an exam situation.

The *Cambridge English: First* exam consists of four tests as follows:

TEST	TIMING	PARTS	FORMAT
READING & USE OF ENGLISH	1 hour 15 minutes	7	Parts 1 to 4 contain tasks with a grammar or vocabulary focus. Parts 5 to 7 contain a range of texts with accompanying reading comprehension tasks.
WRITING	1 hour 20 minutes	2	Part 1 is a compulsory discursive essay. In Part 2, students choose from three different task types which can include an article, an informal or formal email / letter, a review or a report. In the *First for Schools* exam, students may choose a story or a task based on a set text.
LISTENING	approx. 40 minutes	4	Parts 1 and 4 are multiple choice, Part 2 involves sentence completion and Part 3 is a multiple matching task.
SPEAKING	14 minutes	4	Tasks: a short exchange with the interlocutor, a one-minute individual 'long turn', a collaborative task with a fellow candidate and a discussion.

How do I use this book?

This book is divided into three sections: Reading and Use of English, Writing and Speaking. In these parts of the exam, being able to use a range of appropriate lexical items is particularly key. However, the vocabulary items will be useful across all areas of the exam.

- This book consists of 32 stand-alone photocopiable lessons. Use the lessons to supplement your coursebook by providing extra practice of specific exam tasks or topic-related vocabulary input and practice. The lessons provide a variety of activities focussing on developing topic-related vocabulary appropriate to the exam as well as raising awareness of particular lexical foci, such as phrasal verbs, word formation, collocation or affixes.

- Every photocopiable lesson includes a final, clearly signposted **EXAM TASK**. These exam-style activities enable students to use the target vocabulary and functional language in an authentic exam task format. The exam task would also be appropriate for doing as timed exam practice.

- The lessons can be used in any order and require little preparation. The activities are designed to be teacher-led, but are used without separate teachers' notes. Clear instructions are on all the pages, which are all photocopiable.

- The test, part and topic focus are clearly labelled at the top of the page.

- The symbol 🕐 gives a guide lesson length, but please note that timings may vary according to class size and level of language. The final activity in each lesson in the Writing section is a writing task. The lesson length assumes the writing activity is done in class, but these tasks are also ideal to set as homework.

- Handy exam tips remind students of strategies to help them prepare for and cope with the different challenges of the exam. Vocabulary tips clarify frequently confused items or ideas as well as raise awareness of ways to group and record lexical items.

- Where appropriate, students are asked to work in pairs or small groups to generate more language and to engage students further in the tasks.

- The comprehensive answer key at the back of the book provides an explanation of the answers.

The Timesaver series

The Timesaver series provides hundreds of ready-made lessons for all levels, topics and age groups. Other *Timesaver for Exams* titles available include *Practice Tests & Tips for First (FCE)*, *Reading and Use of English for First (FCE)*, *Writing for First (FCE)*, *Speaking for First (FCE)* and *Listening for First (FCE)*.

Face to face

1a **Look at the photos. In which of these situations might someone … ?**

- break the ice
- make small talk
- overhear something

1b **Discuss the questions in pairs.**

a) How can you break the ice when you meet someone for the first time?

b) What can people chat about when they're making small talk?

c) Have you ever delivered a speech? How did it go?

d) Are you a good listener? What could you do to improve?

e) Do you prefer to talk face to face or on the phone?

> **Vocabulary tip!**
>
> *When you're learning new words, record the words they collocate with too, e.g.*
> *to **hold** a conversation*
> *to **make** conversation*

2 **Complete the phrases with the words in the box.**

> deep   endless   fascinating   hold   keeping   making   topic

a) I can just about manage to .... a conversation in French.

b) I think I'm pretty good at .... conversation, though some people say I never stop talking!

c) The weather is a common .... of conversation in the UK.

d) We had a .... conversation about engineering in class today.

e) I'm not very good at .... the conversation going when I meet new people – I always run out of things to say.

f) I didn't want to interrupt them because they seemed to be .... in conversation.

g) We've had .... conversations about politics!

3a **Discuss the statements in pairs. Answer *Yes*, *No* or *It depends*. Give reasons for your answers.**

a) When speaking face to face, you should always make eye contact.

b) Body language reveals to other people how you are feeling.

c) You can't give a great speech if you are nervous.

d) It's OK to interrupt another person.

e) Criticising someone's opinion is OK if you disagree with it.

f) You should never eavesdrop on a private conversation.

3b Now find words in the sentences in exercise 3a which mean the same as these phrasal verbs.

a) listen in on   **b)** give away   **c)** cut in

4 Circle the correct phrasal verbs to complete the sentences.

a) I'm really sorry to **cut** you *down / off / up* while you're speaking, but I need to leave for an appointment.

b) Stop **talking** *down / over / up* **to** me, I'm not a child!

c) Tom's mother **told** him *off / on / out* for breaking the neighbour's window.

d) Why are you **bringing** *across / out / up* that argument again?

e) I'd hoped to **get** my message *across / out / round* in the meeting, but I didn't get a chance to speak!

f) Dad **pointed** *about / out / over* that unless we left for the airport soon, we'd miss our flight.

g) Please **speak** *on / over / up* – I can't hear a word you're saying!

✏️ EXAM TASK: Reading and Use of English (Part 1)

5 For questions 1–8, read the text below and decide which answer (A, B, C or D) best fits each gap.

Making small talk

If you **(0)** *struggle* to make small talk, feel **(1)** .... that you are not alone. Many of us feel **(2)** .... when we meet people for the first time. But there are things you can do to minimise feelings of anxiety.

Let's say you're at your friend's house and they've gone out of the room for a minute, leaving you with their parents. It's polite to **(3)** .... conversation with them, but think of something positive to say rather than worrying that you're going to embarrass yourself. Try not to start thinking negatively, because you might appear nervous or end up **(4)** .... in when someone else is speaking. Your tone of voice might give you away too!

Now let's **(5)** .... you're at a friend's party with some people you don't know. It's important to try to find a **(6)** .... of conversation you're both interested in. Make eye contact, smile and **(7)** .... on whatever it is you all share, like how you know your mutual friend. If talking is still tricky, be a question-asker and a great listener. Then ask follow-up questions to keep the conversation **(8)** ....

0	**A** tackle	**B** fight	**C** struggle	**D** challenge
1	**A** confirmed	**B** guaranteed	**C** assured	**D** settled
2	**A** difficult	**B** awkward	**C** embarrassing	**D** ashamed
3	**A** make	**B** try	**C** do	**D** give
4	**A** putting	**B** getting	**C** starting	**D** cutting
5	**A** create	**B** dream	**C** imagine	**D** believe
6	**A** topic	**B** matter	**C** piece	**D** course
7	**A** discuss	**B** say	**C** mention	**D** comment
8	**A** moving	**B** going	**C** running	**D** passing

Exam tip!

Read the whole text first. Then choose the word which fits in each gap. Often the word you choose instinctively is the correct one! When you have chosen your answers, read through the whole text again and check that it sounds right.

Searching for solutions

1 Look at the photos and discuss in pairs. What issue do all the photos raise?

2a Read the first part of an article below. Which title fits the article best?

> According to **findings** from an environmental group based in New York City, as much as 40 per cent of the food produced in the US never gets eaten. The thrown-out food is worth about 1,500 calories per person per day – almost enough to feed an additional person – and **adds up to** an incredible $165 billion **annually**. 'Some people might **claim** that they don't waste food, but all of us do,' says Elise Golan, a food economist at the U.S. Department of Agriculture in Washington, D.C. 'We just don't pay attention.'
>
> Growing food that ends up being thrown away isn't just wasteful. It **adversely affects** the environment too, using up water and other resources and adding to already overflowing landfills. This food could also be used to help those who don't have enough to eat. All of these factors **have led** experts to search for solutions to fight **widespread** food waste.

a) Specialist solutions **b)** What a waste! **c)** Going hungry

2b Match the words in bold in the text in exercise 2a with the definitions.

a) every year
b) have caused (someone to)
c) information gathered from research or study
d) forms a total of

e) existing in many places and situations
f) has a negative effect on
g) say that something is true even though you cannot prove it

3a Which of the words connected to research is the odd one out in each set?

1	**a)** research	**b)** study	**c)** theory		5	**a)** deny	**b)** maintain	**c)** claim
2	**a)** information	**b)** data	**c)** tips		6	**a)** criticise	**b)** examine	**c)** analyse
3	**a)** effects	**b)** results	**c)** findings		7	**a)** notice	**b)** observe	**c)** comment
4	**a)** prove	**b)** confirm	**c)** propose					

3b Complete the sentences with the words in the box. You may have to change the form of the word.

> analyse   claim   criticise   prove   recommend   theory

Vocabulary tip!

Many words used in academic texts have a less formal equivalent, e.g. propose (more formal) = suggest

a) The study contains some errors and has been widely ....
b) The researcher .... the children's eating habits to find out whether they were eating a balanced diet.
c) The hospital .... that they have reduced food waste but this has not been confirmed.
d) Professor Ronan has a very interesting .... about the origins of our throw-away culture.
e) This research .... beyond all doubt that landfill sites have a negative impact on the environment.
f) The government study finishes with some very useful .... for the future.

4 **Discuss the questions in pairs.**

- Explain your answers to these questions. Would you …

  … buy a damaged packet of food?

  … eat food past its sell-by date?

  … buy fruit and vegetables that don't look perfect?

- How can families and individuals reduce the amount of food they waste?

- Who do you think wastes more food: consumers or companies, e.g. supermarkets?

5a **Read the second part of the article. What solutions have been found to reduce food waste?**

Grocery stores and restaurants are major sources of food waste. They often send back food shipments because they don't look appealing or are slightly damaged. For example, if a refrigerated product arrives even one degree above the recommended temperature, a store can reject it. Damaged cans and packaging can also be refused. At home, people throw out perfectly good food instead of eating leftovers because the sell-by date has passed.

But many of these foods are still nutritious and safe to eat. In an effort to combat this waste, some stores have begun selling imperfect or 'ugly' fruit and other produce at cheaper prices. Others are stocking foods rejected by competitors because they're close to their sell-by dates. Both tactics offer healthy and inexpensive options for people in need. Some smaller store owners work directly with local farmers, fishermen and manufacturers to recover surplus food at low or no cost.

5b **Find a word or words in the text in exercise 5a which mean:**

a) good for you   **b)** having some bad characteristics   **c)** cheap   **d)** more than is needed

---

✏ **EXAM TASK: Reading and Use of English (Part 1)**

6 **For questions 1–8, read the text below and decide which answer (A, B, C or D) best fits each gap.**

Reducing food waste at college

When she was seventeen, Nicola Esposito wanted to **(0)** ____find____ a solution to the food waste problem at the college she attended. First, she **(1)** _____ students and teachers during mealtimes. She **(2)** _____ that they were piling too much food on their plates which they were unable to finish, often leaving the **(3)** _____ , but not so tasty, parts of the meal.

Nicola **(4)** _____ possible solutions to the problem and came up with one or two, such as asking the cafeteria staff to serve smaller portions, and cooking vegetables in a different way. Once she had done this, she **(5)** _____ which solutions would have the greatest impact on reducing waste. Then she asked her classmates for feedback, and asked them to make **(6)** _____ on how her ideas could be improved. Based on what they said, Nicola adjusted her proposals and put them into action.

Later, she collected **(7)** _____ to see whether her solutions had been successful at reducing waste. Her efforts **(8)** _____ in less waste and tastier, healthier meals.

0	**A** look	**B** find	**C** search	**D** hunt
1	**A** viewed	**B** observed	**C** inspected	**D** discovered
2	**A** noticed	**B** watched	**C** caught	**D** examined
3	**A** delicious	**B** imperfect	**C** nutritious	**D** unhealthy
4	**A** looked after	**B** looked around	**C** looked up	**D** looked for
5	**A** regarded	**B** considered	**C** reflected	**D** thought
6	**A** directions	**B** findings	**C** instructions	**D** recommendations
7	**A** theories	**B** knowledge	**C** tips	**D** data
8	**A** finished	**B** concluded	**C** resulted	**D** founded

Exam tip!

*The options will always fit the gap grammatically (e.g. all four options will be verbs), but only one word will fit the **context**. Read the sentence around the gap very carefully.*

Flora and fauna

1   **Work in pairs. Find examples of the classes of animal a–f in the photos and word box.**

a) amphibian   **b)** bird   **c)** crustacean

d) insect   **e)** mammal   **f)** reptile

bat	bear	beetle	chameleon	crab	crocodile	deer	eagle	fox	gorilla
leopard	owl	python	seal	swan	toad	wasp	wolf		

2   **Circle the correct words to complete the sentences.**

a) In the US, over 60% of households have a pet and *domestic / wild* cats are one of the most popular.

b) Polar bears are powerful *predators / prey*.

c) Big cats like tigers are *diurnal / nocturnal* and do their hunting mostly at night.

d) Many land mammals, such as wolves, are very territorial. They will defend their home against other groups of the same *habitat / species*.

e) Even rabbits, which are fairly shy creatures, can display *dominant / submissive* behaviour within their social groups.

3a   **Read the sentences and complete each gap with a word in the box.**

a	and	at	can	have	instead	is	lots	their	them	which

1   A domestic cat can run at .... speed of almost 48 kilometres an hour, which is equivalent to running 100 metres in just 7.5 seconds.

2   Pandas don't sleep in a single chosen place. .... , they fall asleep wherever they are .... the time.

3   Surprisingly, polar bears .... black skin .... their hair isn't white. It's actually transparent.

4   Rabbits, which have .... of predators, have almost 360° vision, which allows .... to detect approaching danger from any direction.

5   When sheep become ill with certain diseases, they self-medicate. In other words, they eat particular plants which .... cure them.

6   The tiger has legs .... are so powerful that the animal can die and remain standing up.

7   When a male Adelie penguin .... choosing a partner, he will offer her a pebble.

8   Some people think that wolves are a threat to humans and .... pets, but in fact, they are very shy.

3b   **Now look at the words you have written and find an example of each of the parts of speech below.**

a) adverb   **e)** main verb   **i)** possessive pronoun

b) auxiliary verb   **f)** modal verb   **j)** relative pronoun

c) conjunction   **g)** preposition   **k)** quantifier

d) definite or indefinite article   **h)** personal pronoun

4a **Look at the list of animals in exercise 1 again and answer the questions.**

- Which animals are typically associated with woodland or forest habitats?
- Which are common in tropical rainforest habitats?

4b **Label the photo with the words in the box.**

berry   bud   flower   leaf
roots   seeds   stem

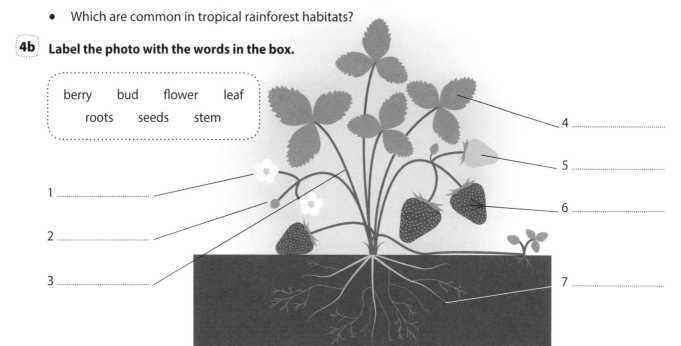

1 ....

2 ....

3 ....

4 ....

5 ....

6 ....

7 ....

✏️ **EXAM TASK: Reading and Use of English (Part 2)**

5 **For questions 1–8, read the text below and think of the word which best fits each gap. Use only one word in each gap. There is an example at the beginning (0).**

Hedgerows: an important habitat

Hedges, or hedgerows as they **(0)** ....*are*........ also known, were originally planted to create boundaries between fields and farms in Britain. In recent years, many of the UK's hedgerows have been removed to make way for housing **(1)** .... to increase field size for larger and more efficient farming machinery. Unfortunately, this has created significant problems for the wildlife **(2)** .... inhabited the areas.

Hedgerows consist **(3)** .... a variety of plants and bushes. These not **(4)** .... provide places for wildlife, such as birds or mice, to make **(5)** .... homes in, but they also provide food, like berries and seeds. Insects collect nectar from flowers growing **(6)** .... in spring too. Hedgerows provide vital links across the countryside for wildlife, helping **(7)** .... to move about freely. Hedgerows also help to prevent soil erosion, **(8)** .... addition to storing carbon which helps fight climate change. They are also valued for their potential to reduce flooding.

Exam tip!

Read the text first to understand the gist and decide what parts of speech are missing. When you have finished writing your answers, read through the text again to check the words fit grammatically.

Extreme conditions

1a   **Work in pairs. Look at the words in the box. Which of these natural disasters are shown in the photos?**

> avalanche   bush fire   earthquake   flooding   hurricane   landslide   tornado   tsunami   volcano

1b   **Think about a natural disaster you have seen on the news. Tell your partner what happened.**

2   **Read the sentences and look at the words in bold. Identify which are *adjectives*, *adverbs*, *nouns* or *verbs*.**

a) During a **volcanic** eruption, ash, gases and rocks can be thrown out of the volcano **violently**, but sometimes lava flows **gently** out in streams instead.

b) The **majority** of bush fires occur in Australia. They are usually **seasonal** events when the weather is hot and dry.

c) One of the most **powerful** earthquakes ever recorded was the Valdivia earthquake which occurred in Chile in May, 1960. It measured a **remarkable** 9.5 on the Richter scale.

d) There are a variety of factors which cause flooding. **Obstruction** of drainage systems, heavy rainfall and ground which has little capacity to absorb water are some of the most common.

e) Tsunami waves can reach **dramatic** heights. It's difficult to predict when a tsunami will occur, though scientists are able to create models which give some **indication** of the course and form they will take.

f) Many landslides are due to **natural** causes, such as heavy rain. When an earthquake occurs, the **movement** of the earth can cause a landslide.

g) Large hurricanes tend to **strengthen** during the night and **weaken** during the day. This is because the atmosphere cools at night, pulling moisture into the hurricane.

h) Tornadoes are rotating columns of air which extend **downwards** from a thunderstorm to the ground. The most violent ones can pull trees out of the ground and move cars hundreds of metres.

3a   **These words from exercise 2 all include suffixes. What is the root of each word?**

a) *volcano* → volcanic   f) .... → powerful   k) .... → natural

b) .... → violently   g) .... → remarkable   l) .... → movement

c) .... → gently   h) .... → obstruction   m) .... → strengthen

d) .... → majority   i) .... → dramatic   n) .... → weaken

e) .... → seasonal   j) .... → indication   o) .... → downwards

3b   **What change in the part of speech has taken place in each case?**

Example: *volcano → volcanic = noun → adjective*

4   **Underline the suffixes on the words in exercise 3a. Which suffixes are used to form *adjectives*, *adverbs*, *nouns* or *verbs*?**

Example: *-ity = noun*

5a Read the text about avalanches. What part of speech is missing from each gap?

AVALANCHES

An avalanche is a sudden **(1)** .... of snow down a mountain. Avalanches are of **(2)** .... danger to people who live in areas where there are high mountains or glaciers. The snow which is loosened by an avalanche can move extremely **(3)** .... down a steep slope, reaching speeds of 130 kph in just five seconds.

The causes of avalanches include heavy snowfall, cutting down of trees, vibrations from earthquakes, loud noises or **(4)** .... who go off-piste. They also occur when fresh snow falls on ice and then slides down or when the wind piles up snow, which drops off mountain edges.

It is crucial to manage avalanches in order to limit the **(5)** .... they cause. Predictions and forecasts can help to **(6)** .... people in mountainous regions of when an avalanche is likely to occur. Snow fences and trees are established and in some cases controlled avalanches are **(7)** .... started to prevent the build-up of snow.

5b Add suffixes to the words in the box to form new words to complete the text in exercise 5a. Are there any different suffixes to add to your lists from exercise 4?

> destroy   intention   move   note   rapid   signify   ski

Vocabulary tip!

Keep a record of words which take the same suffix and look out for any unusual spelling patterns, e.g.
prepare → preparation

✎ EXAM TASK: Reading and Use of English (Part 3)

6 For questions 1–8, read the text below. Use the word given in capitals at the end of some of the lines to form a word that fits in the gap in the same line.

How a tsunami is created

A tsunami is an enormous wave, which is most **(0)** .....*commonly*..... caused by earthquakes or	**COMMON**
volcanic **(1)** .... on the ocean floor. This creates some movements which are so	**ACTIVE**
(2) .... that they displace the water, and it is this which triggers tsunami waves.	**FORCE**
Although they move at **(3)** .... speeds in deep water – around 800 kilometres	**BELIEVE**
per hour – the waves slow towards **(4)** .... areas. At this point, the waves move	**COAST**
closer together and there is a **(5)** .... increase in their height.	**DRAMA**
Often, there is very little warning that a tsunami is about to strike land. Usually, the only **(6)** .... that a tsunami is approaching is that the sea suddenly retreats away from the land. In doing so, large stretches of the beach and seabed are exposed.	**INDICATE**
Tsunamis are hugely **(7)** .... to land and life, and are capable of causing	**DAMAGE**
widespread **(8)** ...., including flooding. Water not only affects homes and buildings, but it also erodes structures such as sea walls, marinas and bridges.	**DESTROY**

Exam tip!

Read the text first. Then think about the part of speech which is needed in each gap. Make the changes required to the word given.

Splash out or save up?

1a **Read what three people say about their money habits and discuss in pairs. Who is:**

a) careful with their money?

b) realistic in their attitude towards money?

c) a bit irresponsible with money?

> When I've got any money, it burns a hole in my pocket. I want to spend it as soon as I get it! I guess I should spend more wisely but life's too short to save for a rainy day, isn't it?

> I don't save every penny, but I do plan for the future and have a savings account. I do splash out sometimes! It's important to treat yourself occasionally. It's all about finding a balance.

> Some people think I'm stingy because I put aside as much as I can. I'm not extravagant, but I do buy good quality items. Buying cheap stuff is a false economy – you have to replace it sooner.

1   **2**   **3**

1b **Match the money words and phrases from exercise 1a with the definitions.**

1	save for a rainy day		**a)**	spend a lot of money on something
2	splash out		**b)**	choose a moderate course of action
3	be extravagant		**c)**	be mean or ungenerous
4	treat yourself		**d)**	be keen to spend his money
5	find a balance		**e)**	spend more than is necessary
6	be stingy		**f)**	buy something special that you will enjoy
7	false economy		**g)**	put money aside for a future time of need
8	money is burning a hole in his pocket		**h)**	an attempt to save money which leads you to spend more money

1c **Discuss in your pairs. Which of the people in exercise 1a do you think has the best attitude? Who are you most like?**

2 **Complete the phrasal verbs related to money with the words in the box.**

> back   by   in   off   on   out   up

a) I'm going to the bank now to pay .... the money I got for my birthday.

b) Sheena's saving .... for a deposit on a house.

c) Could I borrow some cash? I promise I'll pay you .... when I get paid.

d) I can't live .... such a low income. I need to find a better job.

e) I need to go to a cashpoint and take some money ....

f) I'll finish paying .... my loan next month, then I'll have more money to spend!

g) I've been putting some money .... , so we can have a nice holiday this year.

3a   **Circle the correct verb in each sentence.**

a)   Thank you for supporting our charity. You can *get / make* a regular donation by setting up a monthly direct debit.

b)   An increasingly popular way for students to *have / make* a bit of money is to test new products and fill out online surveys about them.

c)   The chances of *getting / making* rich by winning the lottery are very small indeed.

d)   Go on to our website to check your account or *have / make* a payment.

e)   If you *get / make* an investment in a company, the value of your money can go down as well as up.

f)   You can *get / make* money off the ticket if you book early.

3b   **Answer the questions in pairs. Explain your answers.**

Have you:

- recently donated money?
- ever invested money in something?
- ever made a lot of money on something?
- recently got a great discount on something?

> **Vocabulary tip!**
>
> *Sometimes there can be a difference in meaning between words formed from the same root word.*
> The **economy** is very weak at the moment. *(n)*
> My brother is studying **economics** at university. *(pl n)*
> This car isn't very **economical** on fuel. *(adj)*

✎ EXAM TASK: Reading and Use of English (Part 3)

4   **For questions 1–8, read the text below. Use the word given in capitals at the end of some of the lines to form a word that fits in the gap in the same line.**

Money tips from the super-rich

People with a lot of wealth tend to be pretty smart with their money, say **(0)** ....*financial*.... **FINANCE**
advisors. These money experts say that the super-rich make **(1)** .... for the   **INVEST**
future, rather than thinking about what they want right now. **(2)** .... money is   **SAVE**
important and you should plan how much you're going to put aside each month and do it,
rather than being **(3)** .... and spending whatever you want, hoping there'll be   **RESPONSIBLE**
some left over to put in the bank. Wealthy people don't spend all their **(4)** .... ,   **EARN**
and people who retire early are able to do so because they live **(5)** ....   **ECONOMIC**

These people have thought carefully about how they want their lives to be in their
(6) .... and made regular contributions to pension funds over the years.   **RETIRE**
Making regular **(7)** .... into pensions and other funds is easy to do, especially   **PAY**
with online **(8)** .... facilities making these transactions quick and hassle-free.   **BANK**

> **Exam tip!**
>
> *In Part 3, you **must** change the form of the word on the right so that it fits in the gap. You may need to add a prefix or a suffix, change the part of speech, or create a new verb form.*

Making it big!

1a Look at the photos. What are these people's professions?

1b Discuss in pairs. Which of the jobs in the photos would you most like to do? Why?

2a Read about three people who work in the arts and media. What is each person's profession? How does each person hope to make it big?

1 'I started off taking photos, trying to **capture** interesting shots of friends and family, before branching into TV filming. The first time something I'd filmed was broadcast I was really proud of what the whole team had achieved. I'd like to make a name for myself as someone who can not only reproduce a director's vision for a **scene** but take it one step further. I love being on set and getting to work with members of the **cast**. Backstage they're getting into costume and going over their lines. That's the bit viewers never get to see. My ambition is to work on the production team of a Hollywood **blockbuster**, but only a few lucky people ever get that far in the industry.'

2 'I've kept a blog for years, and often post articles on websites, but I'd love to go into fiction and write a bestseller. I've got an idea for the plot of a mystery novel which I'd like to then develop into a series based around the same character. Writing's much harder than people think and creating convincing **dialogue** for a script is something that I personally find tough, so I doubt I'll go into **screenwriting**. If I could find a publisher who liked my idea and would get my novel **published**, I'd be thrilled.'

3 'I often get asked what it is that I actually do. Working in public relations, or PR, means I work on a person's relationship with the public. I work in the film industry, **promoting** actors and entertainers. I help to make sure they make **appearances** at industry events and get noticed by the right people. I get as much publicity for them as possible – photo shoots in magazines, interviews to tie in with a film **release**, advertising work – anything which gets them seen by the public and the media. My dream is to represent a major star.'

2b Match some of the words in bold in the texts in exercise 2a with the definitions.

a) when a record or film is available to buy or see

b) actors in a film, play or show

c) the process of creating a script or adapting a play for cinema

d) conversation in a film, book or play

e) helping someone become successful

f) catch an image of someone or something

3 Read the sentences. Which of the underlined words are incorrect in this context? Replace each of the incorrect words with a word shown in bold in exercise 2a.

a) As a model, I'm used to spending long hours at fashion <u>shoots</u>.

b) Jensen's quite shy – he doesn't really make many public <u>relations</u>.

c) The book's due to be <u>produced</u> on the 23rd of this month.

d) The programme will be <u>broadcast</u> on Channel Six at 7pm.

e) My favourite <u>plot</u> in the whole film was when they were on the plane.

f) The director's new film is a <u>bestseller</u>. It's made $100 million at the box office.

> **Vocabulary tip!**
>
> *Record different ways of saying the same thing, e.g.* become a household name, become well-known, make it big, become a star

4 Find the phrases in exercise 2a which mean the same as the following.

Text 1

a) It would be good to become known for … ....

b) It's great to have the chance to … ....

Text 2

c) I'm pretty sure I won't … ....

d) … is really difficult for me ....

Text 3

e) People frequently ask … ....

f) … the most … I can ....

✏ **EXAM TASK: Reading and Use of English (Part 4)**

5 For questions 1–4, complete the second sentence so that it has a similar meaning to the first sentence, using the word given. Do not change the word given. You must use between two and five words, including the word given.

0 'I don't have an artistic bone in my body,' she said.

SKILLED

She told me that she was *not skilled at* .... art.

1 I had never heard such a good soundtrack before.

EVER

The soundtrack was the .... heard.

2 Do you know the publication date for the new edition of the book?

GOING

Do you know when they .... the new edition of the book?

3 In my opinion, the critic wrote a particularly unfair review.

VERY

I don't think the critic's review .... at all.

4 I found the latest episode of *Mindcatcher* entertaining.

WAS

I .... the latest episode of *Mindcatcher*.

Disaster zone

1a **Match the words with the definitions.**

1	drought	**a)**	when people are extremely poor
2	famine	**b)**	when there is little access to clean water and waste products aren't removed properly
3	poverty	**c)**	when there is no rain for a long time and people don't have enough water
4	war	**d)**	when a lot of people are angry about something within a country
5	civil unrest	**e)**	when people in an area do not have enough food
6	poor sanitation	**f)**	when there is armed fighting between two or more groups or countries

1b **Discuss in pairs. What factors or issues might cause the situations in exercise 1a to occur?**

2 **Read the title and subheading from a magazine article and discuss the questions in your pairs. Then read the extract from the article below and see if your ideas were correct.**

- What was the problem?
- What did Kiara do?
- How do you think Kiara used the oranges?

Fighting drought with oranges

Teenager Kiara Nirghin discovered a way to help South Africa survive a record-breaking drought – in her kitchen

A few years ago, South Africa began experiencing its worst drought in several decades. The lack of frequent rainfall **devastated** crop production. And as the food supply **declined**, most people began to **lose hope**: famine can quickly lead to **starvation**, turning an entire region into a disaster zone. Luckily, 17-year-old Kiara Nirghin isn't like most people.

Instead of being **discouraged** by the problem, the teen **turned her attention to** finding a solution. Kiara began studying the **causes and effects** of drought to see how she could help. 'If you don't understand the problem fully, you won't understand whether or not your solution is **effective**,' she says.

Kiara started thinking of a scientific way to **tackle** the issue. 'There's not much science can do to improve rainfall,' she says. 'So I started looking at research and found that even areas severely affected by drought receive some rain – it just doesn't fall regularly.' She wondered if there was a way to capture those **precious** drops of water and store them in the soil. That way, the water could be released slowly over time to **nourish** crops even during the driest times.

While doing her research, Kiara came across a class of **super-absorbent materials**. They are used in products like babies' nappies to **soak up** liquid. The teen wondered if these substances could help soil hold on to the **moisture** from the little rain that fell. Then crops would have access to water even in dry conditions. Since most of these substances aren't good for the environment, Kiara developed her own non-toxic version made from a simple ingredient – orange peel.

3a **Read the text again and answer the questions using your own words.**

a) How did Kiara react to the drought in South Africa?

b) What did she think it was important to do in order to solve the problem?

c) What did Kiara try to find out about?

3b **Look at the words in bold in the text and discuss in pairs. How many of these words are unfamiliar? Can you work out what they mean from the context (the words around them)? Which two words or phrases describe how people felt?**

4 **Complete the sentences with some of the words or phrases in bold in exercise 2.**

a) You've spilt your coffee all over my desk! Get something to .... , please.

b) I think the baby's swallowed some shampoo, but at least it's ....

c) Numbers of certain wild animals have .... and some are now critically endangered.

d) The medicine the doctor gave me is very .... My cough's almost gone.

e) How are we going to .... the issue of global warming?

5a **Read the next part of the article. Why were experts impressed with Kiara's work?**

Kiara's curiosity led her to research super-absorbent polymers (plastics). The powder form of these **chemicals** can absorb hundreds of times their own weight in liquid. A super-absorbent polymer (SAP) spread in **soil** could, in theory, hold rainwater for plants to use during periods of drought. Unfortunately, most SAPs are expensive and made with chemicals that are toxic to plants and animals. Kiara needed something that was cheap and safe to use. 'You can find these kinds of **molecules** in a lot of natural sources,' she says. 'The best option was something I

23

found in orange peel.' Orange peel (skin) is also biodegradable and able to naturally break down without harming the environment.

Kiara made three orange-peel-based mixtures and tested their absorbing power against three common SAPs. She performed three experiments. The first tested water absorption. The second examined the ability of the **substances** to maintain soil moisture over a three-week period. And the last looked at how well the materials helped an actual plant survive in drought conditions. A homemade

mixture of orange peel, avocado skin, and lemon juice came out on top. It beat Kiara's other mixtures, as well as commonly-used SAPS.

Experts at the Google Science Fair were very impressed with Kiara's work. But although we might think her achievements are extraordinary, she says that anyone can do what she's done. All you need to do is believe in yourself, stay curious and keep experimenting. 'It's never too early to start doing science,' says Kiara. 'Even if you're young, you still have the ability to create something world-changing.'

5b **Match the words in bold in the text with the definitions.**

1	chemical	a)	a solid, liquid or gas
2	soil	b)	something used in or produced through chemistry
3	substance	c)	the top layer of earth that plants grow in
4	molecule	d)	the smallest unit of a solid, liquid or gas

🖉 **EXAM TASK: Reading and Use of English (Part 5)**

6 **For questions 1–3, choose the answer (A, B, C or D) which you think fits best according to the text in exercise 5a.**

1 When Kiara was researching materials, she
   A looked for something that would not cause harm.
   B considered a number of inexpensive SAPS.
   C started by looking at things she already had.
   D hoped to create a new kind of plastic.

Exam tip!

The words in the four options will not be the same as those in the text. Learning synonyms will help you prepare for this.

2 What does *power* mean in line 23?
   A amount
   B depth
   C force
   D ability

3 In the final paragraph, we learn that Kiara
   A wished she had started her research sooner.
   B did not believe she deserved to win an award.
   C did not think what she had done was incredible.
   D never imagined her work would have such an impact.

Going plastic-free

1 Look at the photo and discuss in pairs. What does the image show?

2a Read the title and subheading for a magazine article. What information do you expect to find out from reading the article?

Should plastic bags be banned?

They're bad for the Earth, but are the alternatives any better? Two leading writers on environmental issues bring us their opinions.

2b Read one writer's view in the first part of the article. What does the writer think about the use of plastic bags?

YOU SEE THE DIFFERENCE A TURTLE DOES NOT.

©2014 MEDASSET

Paper or plastic? It might not seem like a significant choice to make at the supermarket check-out. The **impact** of this decision, **(1)** .... , can be enormous. The estimated five trillion plastic bags which are **discarded** each year across the world cause serious ocean and soil pollution. In the Los Angeles area of the US alone, 10 tons of plastic are carried into the Pacific Ocean every day. On land and at sea, these **accumulate** and become a **hazard** for wildlife, and they have polluted waters as far away as the Arctic Ocean.

To make a bad situation even worse, plastic bags often end up in landfill, where they eventually **break down** into tiny pieces. These can easily blow into oceans and drains that feed into bodies of water. **(2)** .... the plastic breaks down, **toxins** can be released which **contaminate** soil and water, prevent plant growth and make water undrinkable.

(3) .... recycling could help to reduce the problem, recycling **regulations** can make it difficult and expensive to sort and process different types of plastic. According to research, only 13.5 per cent of plastic bags were recycled in 2013.

(4) .... we start taking steps to promote positive change, we are facing an environmental **catastrophe**. One of the best **strategies** is to **opt for** reusable bags instead of single-use alternatives. This is something more shoppers will be **forced** to do **(5)** .... there are more plastic bag bans in place. It's up to us to make the right choices and push for change in our communities. **(6)** .... we can learn to prevent the problems that come with plastic, we'll be taking a bold and important step to creating a better, safer planet.

3 Read the article again and complete the gaps using words from the box. There is more than one possible answer for some of the items.

> as   if   once   though   unless   when   whereas   while

Vocabulary tip!

Record phrases to remind you how conjunctions are used, e.g. I'm going to avoid using plastic **now (that)** I'm aware of the issue.

4a Look at the words in bold in the article. Are they used as nouns or verbs?

4b Now match the words in bold in the text with the synonyms below.

Paragraph 1:	**a)** build up	**b)** danger	**c)** effect	**d)** thrown away
Paragraph 2:	**a)** decay	**b)** pollute	**c)** poisons	**d)** rules
Paragraph 3:	**a)** choose	**b)** disaster	**c)** made to	**d)** plans

5 Read the second part of the article below and discuss the questions in your pairs. Does the second writer have the same opinion? Who do you think makes the best argument?

6 Find words and phrases in this part of the article which match the definitions.

a) a place where waste is buried under the ground

b) the measurement of carbon dioxide produced

c) aware

d) a gas produced when carbon is burned

e) causing or likely to cause damage

f) a chemical used to kill insects

g) able to be used again

h) the process of making or growing things to be sold

> **Exam tip!**
>
> In Part 6, you will read a text with **six** missing sentences. Read the whole text first. Next, read the options and look for clues in the sentences around the gaps in the text.

✎ EXAM TASK: Reading and Use of English (Part 6)

7a Read the second part of the magazine article again. Some sentences have been removed from the article. Choose from the sentences A–E the one which fits each gap (1–4). There is one extra sentence which you do not need to use.

Plastic bags may be harmful to the environment. **1**☐ What we should really be asking ourselves is whether there are actually some advantages to keeping plastic bags around, and whether those benefits outweigh the harm. **2**☐ In addition, research has indicated that these have a higher carbon footprint than plastic ones because it takes more energy to produce and transport them. Even reusable cotton bags, which the environmentally-conscious amongst us might opt for, are not necessarily a better option.

It takes many thousands of litres of water and a significant number of pesticides to produce a kilo of cotton, and although cotton bags last longer than plastic or paper ones, they too will eventually end up in landfill sites. **3**☐ Like it or not, it looks as though plastic bags may still be better than the alternatives. According to some experts, plastic bags cause less stress on the environment because their production uses less water, requires fewer chemicals and emits fewer greenhouse gases, which means their carbon footprint is half that of cotton or paper bags. **4**☐ There must be more efficient ways to reduce waste: and it's up to us to figure out what they are.

A   So, while it sounds like a good idea in theory, attempting to ban plastic bags completely is unrealistic.

B   People are starting to switch to paper bags, thinking they are better for the environment, when, in fact, millions of trees must be cut down to manufacture them.

C   This amounts to around 0.2 per cent of the total waste generated in the US in 2013.

D   Because they are quite thick, they take up a lot of space there, whereas much thinner plastic bags require significantly less.

E   The effects of banning them, though, would be even more so.

7b Once you have made your choices, re-read the whole article to check that they make sense in context.

Video game craze

1a The text below is the first part of an article. Read the title of the article. What is the article about? What does 'conquered the world' mean? Read the text quickly to check your answers.

1b Read the first part of the article. Find synonyms for the following words in the text.

a) craze (n)   b) fan (n)   c) goal (n)   d) imaginary (adj)

e) original (adj)   f) player (n)   g) release (n)   h) was released (v)

The games that conquered the world

They wandered in groups, their eyes glued to their phones. They walked slowly, zigzagging through streets, wandering through national parks, and hanging around in front of strangers' homes. They were players of *Pokémon GO* when it was brought out in July 2016. Entrepreneur John Hanke thought that enthusiasts of *Pokémon*, which started out as a video game in 1996, would love a new kind of game. He was right. Within ten days of its launch, the mobile app was downloaded by 15 million people. **[1]** . In some ways, it did.

The object of *Pokémon GO* is simple: to find and capture fictional creatures known as Pokémon which are hiding outside in your neighbourhood. The augmented reality feature of the game allows you to see the creatures in your actual environment, making the game personal to the user. The ultimate aim of the game is to collect all the Pokémon which may also be used to battle those of an opponent.

[2] Another innovative feature was the promotion of physical exercise. *Pokémon GO* got millions of people outdoors. In the early days, most people played the game with friends, and got exercise while they were doing it. Playing the game wasn't always safe, though. **[3]** This led to Hanke's team working on improving the safety of the game. In its first year, the app was downloaded 750 million times worldwide, and an estimated 10% of all mobile phones in the US had the app installed. Though the peak of the *Pokémon GO* trend has now passed, playing figures continue to be impressive.

2a Complete the gaps with the three sentences (A–C) which have been removed.

A It was this combination of the player's real world with the cartoon world of *Pokémon*, a mix of fact and fantasy, that made the game so **unlike** others at the time.

B In its initial few months, distracted players **not only** walked into traffic **but also** stumbled off bridges and even fell off cliffs.

C The game was **a great deal more** popular than many other video games had been, and many people believed it would forever change the way video games were played.

> **Vocabulary tip!**
>
> *Print out an interesting article and blank out one or two sentences. Then swap texts with a partner and see if they can guess what information is in the missing sentences.*

2b Look at the words and phrases in bold in sentences A–C in exercise 2a. What is the function of these phrases?

3 Complete the sentences with the words and phrases in the box.

a) This console is much smaller .... the previous version.

b) The quality of the graphics in the latest games is .... to those in early games.

c) The gameplay in original video games was basic, ... today people's expectations are much higher.

d) Early video games were .... complex than the latest games which have huge development budgets.

e) In this game you .... need good hand-eye coordination, but also fast reactions.

f) .... many players, I prefer strategy games to action games.

✏️ **EXAM TASK: Reading and Use of English (Part 6)**

4 **You are going to read the second part of the article. Four sentences have been removed from this part of the article. Choose from the sentences D–G the one which fits each gap (4–6). There is one extra sentence which you do not need to use.**

4 ☐ Today *Pong* seems like a very basic match of ping pong played on a TV screen. But on its launch on a September morning in 1972, a crowd of people got up early to line up outside a gaming arcade in Sunnyvale, California, for the chance to play the innovative game.

Pong was invented by a maths expert called Nolan Bushnell. As a college student, he spent long hours alone working in the computer lab. **5** ☐ It could take hours for them to complete a single problem. Students like Bushnell needed something fun to do while they waited. Bushnell passed a lot of time playing a computer game called *Spacewar*. But the game was difficult to play unless you were a maths whizz. **6** ☐ The directions were just one line: 'Avoid missing ball for high score.' *Pong* became a huge hit in arcades. A few years later, Bushnell's company, Atari, released a version that could be played on a TV set at home. *Pong* was a simple game – two lines and a dot on a screen. But Bushnell had changed everything: the video game industry had begun. And, as the popularity of games like *Pokémon GO* demonstrate, it hasn't stopped evolving since.

D	He wanted to create a game that, in contrast, anyone could play, and after several attempts, he came up with *Pong*.	**F**	One difference which stands out is the technology used in each of the games.
E	Computers were extremely slow in comparison with today.	**G**	*Pokémon GO* is an incredibly sophisticated game, whereas *Pong*, the first commercially successful video game, was significantly simpler.

---

5 **Read the whole text again. In your pairs, compare and contrast the two video games, *Pokémon GO* and *Pong*. Use the phrases in the box to help you.**

both	not nearly as … as …	compared to
on the other hand	far more … than …	unlike

Exam tip!

Look carefully at linking words and comparisons. They may help you choose the correct sentence for each gap.

6 **Discuss the questions in your pairs.**

- Would you describe yourself as a gamer?
- Have you ever downloaded a new game on the day of its release?
- What's your favourite video game? What's the aim of it?
- What do you do to pass the time, on long journeys, for example?

Outside your comfort zone

1a Look at the list of experiences and discuss in pairs. Have you done or would you like to do any of these? How did / would each of these experiences make you feel? Why? Use the adjectives in the box.

- doing a bungee jump
- going travelling on your own
- riding a motorbike
- giving a talk to a large group of people
- trying some unusual food
- taking part in a TV talent contest
- going to the cinema alone
- getting a completely different haircut
- giving your opinions in a class or meeting
- facing up to a fear or phobia

> cautious   cheerful   determined   enthusiastic   nervous   relaxed   terrified   thrilled   uneasy   unsure

1b Which adjectives in the box express positive feelings? Which express negative feelings? Can you think of synonyms for each word?

2a Complete the sentences with the words in the box. In your pairs, discuss the meaning of the phrases in bold.

> comfort   drawn   felt   push   rush

1 I had my first driving lesson last week. I was really worried because I'd never driven before. I was completely **outside of my** .... **zone**.

2 I .... **empowered** the first time I gave a speech. It was at a wedding. I feel so much more confident about speaking in public now.

3 You've got to .... **yourself** if you want to be brilliant. No one gets a top job without working hard!

4 I love watching thrillers. I get such an **adrenaline** .... I think being a bit scared is exciting!

5 It's really interesting that so many people are so .... **to** extreme sports. I guess they need to experience a sense of danger in their lives.

2b Now find a synonym in the sentences for the adjectives below.

a) bold   **b)** fascinating   **c)** concerned   **d)** thrilling   **e)** amazing

3 Answer these questions in your pairs using words and phrases from exercises 1 and 2.

a) Can you describe a time when you stepped outside your comfort zone? How did you feel?

b) What makes you feel empowered? Why?

c) Do you enjoy pushing yourself? Why? / Why not?

d) What do you get an adrenaline rush from?

e) Are you drawn to doing things which involve taking risks?

Exam tip!

Look for the section of the text which clearly answers each question. Don't rely on matching similar words in the questions and text, as this may lead you to the wrong conclusion!

✎ EXAM TASK: Reading and Use of English (Part 7)

4 You are going to read an article about why people do extreme sports. For questions 1–10, choose from the sections (A–E). The sections may be chosen more than once.

In which paragraph does the writer

explain what might happen when part of our body is not working well? **1** ___

highlight the benefits that doing sports provides? **2** ___

mention how she found out what she was capable of? **3** ___

suggest that we might always wonder about our abilities if we don't take action? **4** ___

describe the effects of a physical reaction? **5** ___

mention a popular belief that if we don't take risks, we won't achieve anything? **6** ___

point out who especially benefits from doing extreme sports? **7** ___

say we should not be put off attempting an activity because of safety concerns? **8** ___

explain the reason we experience a particular response to what's happening? **9** ___

say that achieving something difficult leads to a significant change in how we feel? **10** ___

A   Exciting activities like snowboarding and rock-climbing are sky-rocketing in popularity. Not only does taking risks teach you to be bold, but stepping outside of your comfort zone can make you feel empowered, even if you don't get it right first time. Extreme sports are particularly good for young people who are eager to learn and perfect new passions. Learning to snowboard at the age of eight, I have loved every bit of sport I've done since. Being on the slopes day in, day out helped me gain an understanding of the way my body works: I learned which muscles were responsible for which movements, figured out how to adjust my technique to avoid injury, and discovered my physical limitations. Snowboarding taught me how to push myself, even when I was anxious about falling. And it made me more persistent: one way or another, you always have to make it to the bottom of the slope!

B   There are numerous positives of taking part in sporting activities. It can teach us patience, control and discipline, and participating in activities which require physical exertion means we keep in shape too. Sport also introduces you to a positive community of people who find the same activities interesting and are always willing to help you improve. And the adrenaline rush we get from an extreme sport is good for us. Indeed, there are studies which show that conquering physical feats which scare you – such as surfing a massive wave – can transform your overall confidence.

C   Of course, even the best extreme athletes get injured from time to time, but being bothered about injury should never prevent anyone from doing something they love. With appropriate gear and patience, it is possible to minimize the risk of hurting yourself and benefit from everything extreme sport has to offer. If you don't try, you'll never know how good you could have been. Taking risks and experimenting with new challenges is an appealing thing to do – but why are we so drawn to extreme sports?

D   It could be down to the human body exhibiting a primal response to danger. When you're about to take a risk – like launching yourself down a black run on your snowboard – your body releases adrenaline. This 'fight or flight' hormone prepares your body either to feel confident enough to perform the task or flee from danger. Adrenaline optimizes your blood vessels and air passageways to increase your heart rate and fuel the body's major muscle groups with maximum efficiency. The result is a thrilling combination of turbo-charged speed, strength and endurance.

E   It is widely believed that our bodies developed the fight or flight response millions of years ago, when we were faced with dangers every day, such as encountering ferocious animals while out hunting for food. There is a drawback to all this adrenaline pumping round our system: while your body powers your muscles, it neglects to supply your brain. Without the ability to think in a sensible way in scary moments, you're more prone to taking unwise risks, which could have undesirable consequences. Then again, becoming good at most of life's endeavours requires taking risks. As the saying goes, 'nothing ventured, nothing gained'!

In the workplace

1 **Look at the photos and discuss the questions in pairs.**

- What jobs do the photos show?
- What do the jobs involve?
- Do you know anyone who does these jobs?

2a **Match the words to make job titles. What do these people do?**

1	chief	**a**	rep
2	fire	**b**	analyst
3	business	**c**	servant
4	civil	**d**	executive
5	estate	**e**	guard
6	sales	**f**	agent
7	life	**g**	fighter

> **Vocabulary tip!**
>
> *A compound noun is typically made up of two words, acting as a single noun and can be written as one word* (newsagent), *two words* (taxi driver) *or with a hyphen* (decision-maker). *Use your dictionary to check the most common spelling.*

2b **In your pairs, discuss the pros and cons of each of the jobs in exercise 2a. Think about:**

- financial reward
- level of responsibility
- benefits of the job (e.g. company car)
- decision-making
- hours of work

2c **Discuss in your pairs. Do any of the jobs appeal to you? Which job would you least like to do? Why?**

3a **Read about three people's jobs. Which person:**

has to cope with a high level of stress in her job? **1** ☐

finds the hours she works challenging? **2** ☐

understands that some people wouldn't like the tasks she has to do? **3** ☐

A   Michaela

I'm a machine operator in a factory which manufactures sports shoes. My **income**'s not bad and I have a good **relationship** with my manager and co-workers, which definitely makes time go faster. The main **drawback** is the **shift work** which upsets your routine. There's the chance of **overtime** most weeks, so I can make more money if I want to. I almost always say yes!

I'm an office worker in an accounts department. I enjoy it and there's always plenty to do. I mainly input data into **databases** and **spreadsheets**. Some people don't enjoy admin, but I don't mind it at all. I'm also in charge of the **payroll**, which can be a bit more complicated, but it's a good skill to have.

B   Arlene

I work in IT and regularly have to run the system **backups** which means making sure everything is saved onto the servers. There are strict **deadlines** to stick to for this which can put you under a lot of pressure. I also provide **desktop support** for the people based in our **headquarters**. The IT department always seeks **feedback** for the services we provide, to ensure we're working well with the various departments around the company.

C Gemma

3b **Match some of the nouns in bold in each text with the definitions.**

Text A

a) a system where different workers work at different times of the day or night

b) time spent working after the usual working day

c) the amount of money someone earns from working

d) the way people feel and behave towards each other

Text B

e) a computer program that helps you do financial calculations and planning

f) a large amount of information stored on a computer system which can easily be looked at

Text C

g) a time or day by which something must be done

h) information or opinions which tell you whether something is successful or popular

i) the main offices of an organisation or company

3c **What do the other words in bold in the texts mean? Try to work them out by reading the context carefully. Use your dictionary if necessary.**

Exam tip!

In Part 7, you can read the questions first, so you know what information you're looking for. Some people prefer to read the texts first – it doesn't really matter which way you do this task!

✎ **EXAM TASK: Reading and Use of English (Part 7)**

4 **For questions 4–10, choose from the texts A–C in exercise 3a and text D below. The texts may be chosen more than once.**

Which person

says she wants to make sure everything runs smoothly for the whole organisation? | **4** |

takes every opportunity to increase her earnings? | **5** |

has to deal with people who don't take her work seriously? | **6** |

mentions that she has a variety of easier and more challenging responsibilities? | **7** |

takes an interest in the clients she works for? | **8** |

says that she gets on well with her colleagues? | **9** |

is interested in finding out what people think of the work she does? | **10** |

D Anika

I work as an estate agent, which means showing people around properties. On the plus side, I get to see a lot of really great houses, and pick up a lot of design ideas for my own home. It's fascinating to see how other people live! Occasionally I get a time-waster – someone who just wants to be nosey and have a look round someone else's house. That's frustrating. Generally, though, it's a great job and I meet some really interesting people!

Culture club

culture (n): the beliefs, way of life and customs of a particular people or society

1 The words and phrases in the box are all associated with the culture of a community, such as a country or region. Complete the sentences using one of the words or phrases in the box.

> customs and traditions   beliefs   values   habits and behaviour
>
> language   dress   arts   food   manners

a) Without .... , such as having firework displays at New Year, communities wouldn't have a strong sense of identity.

b) It's very important to respect other people's .... , even if their views are very different from your own.

c) A person's choice of .... communicates important information about who they are and how they wish to be regarded by others, even before you've heard them speak.

d) Before travelling abroad, you should find out what is considered good .... , such as leaving a little food on your plate to indicate you have had enough to eat.

e) Strong moral .... are crucial in maintaining a sense of knowing who we are and what we believe in.

f) The .... allow us to express creativity in a way that other areas of our lives do not.

g) Our .... choices may suggest something about our personalities; for example, some say people who like spicy snacks enjoy taking risks!

h) Some people say that .... defines our identity and helps us feel we belong to a group.

i) Your way of life is the .... that are typical for you.

2 Work in pairs. Choose three of the words or phrases from exercise 1. Tell each other what these are like in your country or region or in another country or region you are familiar with.

3 Add the suffixes *-al* and *-ally* to the words below, making any necessary changes.

a) experiment   *experimental*   *experimentally*

b) economy   ....

c) history   ....

d) law   ....

e) logic   ....

f) nature   ....

g) occasion   ....

> **Vocabulary tip!**
>
> *Look at the word family for* culture*. Notice how suffixes change the part of speech.*
>
> culture *(n)*   cultur**al** *(adj)*   cultur**ally** *(adv)*

4 Complete phrases 1–8 with *culture*, *cultural* or *culturally*. Then match the phrases with their definitions (a–h).

1 .... acceptable

2 .... conflicts

3 .... diversity

4 .... stereotype

5 .... shock

6 .... awareness

7 .... misunderstanding

8 .... significant

a) having an understanding of the differences between your own culture and that of other people

b) important within a particular culture

c) approved of or considered normal within a culture

d) a feeling of confusion felt by someone visiting a country or place they do not know

e) when a word, gesture or idea has different meanings in different cultures

f) a fixed (often incorrect) idea about what a person from a particular culture is like

g) disagreement between people with opposing opinions or principles in a particular community

h) a variety of cultures in a society

5 Discuss the questions in pairs.

- What stereotypes do you think people have of your culture? Do you think there is any truth in them or do you think they are unfair?

- Have you ever been in a cultural situation where you weren't sure how to behave? What happened? If not, what would you do if you weren't sure how to behave in a new place?

✎ EXAM TASK: Writing (Part 1)

6 Write your answer in 140–190 words in an appropriate style.

In your English class, you have been talking about different cultures. Now your English teacher has asked you to write an essay.

Write an essay using **all** the notes and give reasons for your point of view.

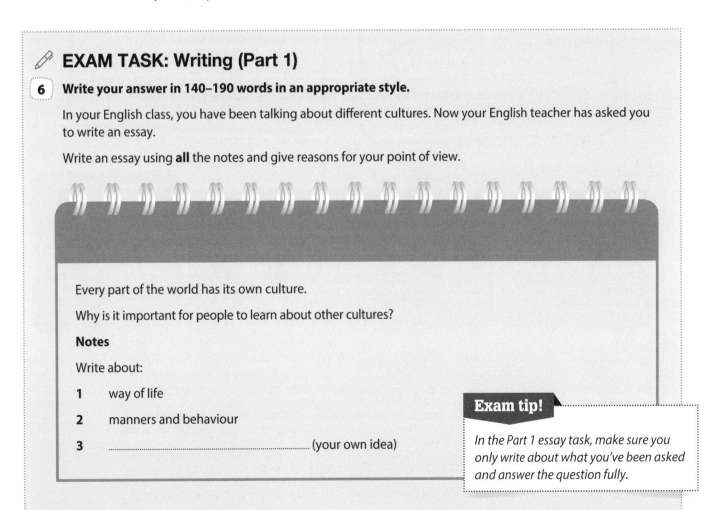

Every part of the world has its own culture.

Why is it important for people to learn about other cultures?

Notes

Write about:

1 way of life

2 manners and behaviour

3 .... (your own idea)

Exam tip!

In the Part 1 essay task, make sure you only write about what you've been asked and answer the question fully.

How well do you know yourself?

1a   Read about two different personality types: parrot and eagle. Which do you think is which?

1

....

You're self-assured and fearless and people love to follow your lead!

Every group needs a leader and whether you're captain of the soccer team or in charge of a group assignment, that person is you. People admire your clear and confident way of speaking and your great ideas.

2

....

You're the life of the party and you can always get a crowd laughing!

You are chatty and fun, so you tend to have friends from different groups. Consider yourself lucky – not everyone has such an easy time getting along with people. You tend to live in the moment and love nothing better than a spontaneous invite.

1b   Underline the personality adjectives in the texts. What do they mean?

2   Read about two more personality types. Then find the personality adjectives in the texts and use some of them to complete the sentences. There may be more than one possible answer.

OWL

You're careful and thorough, always putting your mind to work.

You're all about taking your time, thinking carefully about what you're doing and working hard to get everything exactly right. People like studying or working with you because they know you won't stop until everything's perfect!

DOVE

You're calm, kind and very easy-going. No wonder your friends adore you!

You are the kind of person everyone likes. You're helpful, never bossy and don't like conflict. You go along with whatever the group wants and the world would be a better place if everyone was as caring and thoughtful as you!

a) Jake's so ....! He's always telling people what to do.

b) I'm generally quite a .... person. Nothing really makes me angry or upset.

c) Sandie's very .... with things – you'll never see her break anything or get dirty!

d) Thank you so much for the flowers! You're such a .... person.

e) I'm very .... I'll work hard on something until I know every detail is right.

f) Amit's so .... He's the best person to talk to if you're worried about something.

g) Thanks for doing the dishes for me – it was really ....

3a Read the four descriptions again and discuss in pairs. What's your personality type? Does your partner agree with you?

3b Read this quote from Merrick Rosenberg, a personality expert. A changeable person who you can't trust is sometimes described as a chameleon. How does Merrick use the word differently? Do you agree with her opinion?

> *'We all have shades of all four personality types, and the most successful people know how to bring out different traits depending on the situation – like a chameleon.'*

4a Read the definitions and complete the vowels in the adjectives.

a) giving support or encouragement — s _ p p _ r t _ v _

b) finds it difficult to make decisions — _ n d _ c _ s _ v _

c) able to think of new and interesting ideas — _ m _ g _ n _ t _ v _

d) not frightened of taking risks — b _ l d

e) taking care to avoid risks and danger — c _ _ t _ _ _ s

f) easily annoyed or wanting things to happen quickly — _ m p _ t _ _ n t

g) showing concern for other people and their feelings — c _ n s _ d _ r _ t _

h) able to think calmly and sensibly — r _ t _ _ n _ l

i) enjoys meeting and spending time with people — s _ c _ _ b l _

j) having a lot of energy and enthusiasm — _ n _ r g _ t _ c

> **Vocabulary tip!**
>
> *It can be difficult to remember the correct prefix to make opposite adjectives. If you're really not sure, use 'not very' to get your message across instead, e.g. He's not very considerate.*

4b Make opposite adjectives by adding or removing a prefix to the adjectives in exercise 4a. Which three adjectives do not take a prefix? Think of opposites for these three adjectives.

✎ EXAM TASK: Writing (Part 1)

5 Write your answer in 140–190 words in an appropriate style.

In your English class, you have been talking about friends and relationships. Now, your English teacher has asked you to write an essay.

Write an essay using **all** the notes and give reasons for your point of view.

Friends can be more important than family.

Do you agree?

Notes

Write about:

1 having a similar personality

2 talking about problems

3 .... (your own idea)

> **Exam tip!**
>
> *Make sure you use all the notes and don't forget to include your own idea!*

Setting off

1a Work in pairs. Which of the verbs in the box can be used with these nouns? There is more than one possible answer.

> collect   download   call   arrive   board   go through   make   pack   check in

a) .... a plane

b) .... a taxi

c) .... your luggage

d) .... an online booking

e) .... a boarding pass / an e-ticket

f) .... at the airport

g) .... a suitcase

h) .... at your destination

i) .... passport control / customs / security

1b Discuss in your pairs. What are the people doing in each photo? What other things do they need to do at the airport? Use the phrases in exercise 1a to help you.

2a Which verbs in exercise 1a can be replaced with:

- get on?
- pick up?

2b Complete the sentences with one of the following verbs: *pull out, pull over, pull up*.

a) She was driving too fast on the motorway and a traffic cop .... her ....

b) The ambulance .... at the school gates and the medical team jumped out.

c) I didn't see the other car. It was such a shock! It just .... in front of me.

3 Read two people's decriptions of memorable trips. Complete the texts, using the prepositions in the word box. There is more than one possible answer.

> around   away   back   in   off   out   over   to   up

Vocabulary tip!

A verb can sometimes take different particles to make phrasal verbs with different meanings. Keep a record of phrasal verbs like this.

I went to Madrid on a business trip with a colleague last summer. We couldn't wait to **(1)** get .... from the office for a few days. Once we were **(2)** dropped .... at our hotel, we **(3)** checked .... and then went to find out about the local transport and facilities. Fortunately, we'd packed small carry-on bags as our suitcases didn't **(4)** turn .... until the next day! We spent most of our time in meetings, though we did go into the local town to **(5)** look .... We might be **(6)** going .... to the same hotel next year and I'm really **(7)** looking forward .... it.

PHOTOCOPIABLE

I had an exhausting journey when I moved to Australia with my family to live. We **(8)** set .... at five in the morning and our parents came to **(9)** see us .... at the airport. The kids were a bit nervous about flying for the first time but as we **(10)** picked .... speed along the runway, they started to get pretty excited. We **(11)** stopped .... in Hong Kong for a night which was interesting but very tiring. None of us slept very well. Our final flight eventually **(12)** got .... 36 hours after we **(13)** took .... And we **(14)** stepped .... the plane and into a new adventure!

4 **Complete the sentences with phrasal verbs from exercises 1–3. You may need to change the tense of the verb.**

a) If your luggage doesn't .... , it means that it fails to arrive.

b) My train was half an hour late – we didn't .... until nine-thirty.

c) My boyfriend .... me .... at the airport. He always comes to wave goodbye.

d) Dad .... us .... at the station in his car. We would've missed our train otherwise.

e) Are you .... anywhere on your way to Japan? It'll be nice to break up the journey.

f) I'm .... very early tomorrow morning, so I'll get my things ready now.

g) Are you .... meeting your new customer? You haven't met her before, have you?

h) I don't always have time to .... a new place when I'm there on business.

5 **Discuss these questions in pairs.**

- Have you ever travelled by air? What do / would you like or dislike about air travel?
- How often do you travel by rail, sea or road? Which do you prefer? Why?
- Describe a memorable journey you have made, using some of the vocabulary in this lesson.

✏ EXAM TASK: Writing (Part 1)

6 **Write your answer in 140–190 words in an appropriate style.**

In your English class, you have been talking about travel and transport. Now your English teacher has asked you to write an essay.

Write an essay using **all** the notes and give reasons for your point of view.

Some people say that the best way to travel is the one that gets you there the quickest.

Do you think this is true?

Notes

Write about:

1   forms of transport

2   length of journey

3   .... (your own idea)

Exam tip!

Read the notes you are given and think about how they link to the essay title. Then think of a third point and decide what you will say about it. Planning will help you write a better essay more quickly!

75 mins

Getting away from it all

1 Work in pairs. Read the text and discuss the questions. What kind of text is it? Would you like to do any of the activities mentioned?

Are you tired of the daily commute to class or work? Sick of spending your evenings on essays or reports?

If this sounds familiar, perhaps it's time to **get away from it all** for a week or two. Why not hop on a flight and go trekking in the Himalayas, sail across the ocean on a yacht, or cycle through Europe stopping at fascinating places along the way? Or perhaps you'd prefer to **take it easy** and relax by the pool in an **exotic location**, or go diving in Australia's Great Barrier Reef. Whatever you've got in mind for your **Dream Holiday**, we can help!

We'll organise your **trip of a lifetime** so that you don't have to. Call us today to discuss your requirements, or book one of our luxury **package tours** online.

Got a dream? We'll see you there!

2 Look at the phrases in bold in the text. What do they mean? Match the phrases with their definitions.

1	get away from it all	a)	an unusual or exciting place, far away from home
2	take it easy	b)	the perfect holiday
3	exotic location	c)	escape from your daily routine
4	dream holiday	d)	a holiday you will probably only do once
5	trip of a lifetime	e)	a holiday organised by a travel company for a fixed price
6	package tour	f)	relax

3a Complete the crossword with the different kinds of holiday. Find the answers by reading the definitions or looking at the photo clues.

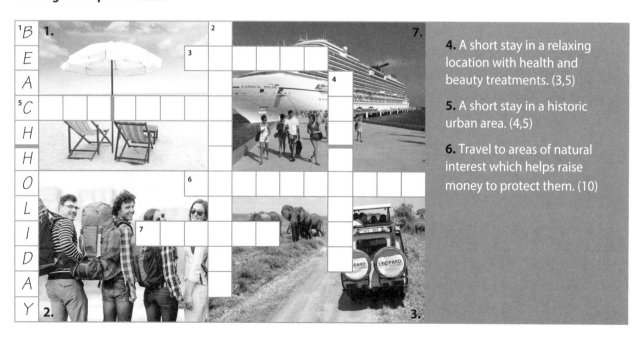

4. A short stay in a relaxing location with health and beauty treatments. (3,5)

5. A short stay in a historic urban area. (4,5)

6. Travel to areas of natural interest which helps raise money to protect them. (10)

PHOTOCOPIABLE

3b **Discuss in your pairs.**

- Have you ever been on any of the holidays in the crossword? Did you enjoy the holiday? Why? / Why not?

- Which kind of holiday would you like to try? Why?.

4a **Read a student's answer to an exam task. What three questions do you think the student was asked to answer?**

*My dream holiday would be to **go on a tour** of Australia. I've wanted to go there since I was a kid and my uncle showed me some photos of the Great Barrier Reef. Australia's a huge country, and there's a lot to see.*

*I'd love to go on an **excursion** to Uluru – an enormous rock which is a sacred place for people. I think there'd be some **stunning scenery** there. I'd also want to try surfing at Bondi beach. The other thing I'd like to do is climb the Sydney Harbour Bridge. I know it's quite a **touristy** thing to do but the views from the top must be spectacular.*

*The person I'd most like to **go away** with is my friend, Lukas. He's really organised, so he'd be amazing at putting together **an itinerary** and making sure we make the flights on time!*

4b **Complete the sentences using the words and phrases in bold from the text. Make any necessary changes.**

a) Do you fancy going on any of the ....? I'd like to see those ruins the tour guide mentioned.

b) When I go on holiday, I like to do all the .... things – even though the places are often crowded!

c) I think we ought to plan .... Otherwise we won't manage to fit everything in.

d) Are you .... on holiday anywhere nice this year?

e) Wow! What .... ! I've never seen anything like it.

f) I wouldn't mind .... of the US. We could travel through all 50 states!

5 **Work in small groups. Discuss the questions.**

- Where would you go for your dream holiday?

- Do you prefer to go on holiday abroad or stay in your own country?

- Which places in your country are most popular with tourists?

- Which places in your country would you (not) recommend to visitors?

Exam tip!

Read through your answer and check you have addressed all the questions in the task.

✎ EXAM TASK: Writing (Part 2)

6 **Write your answer in 140–190 words in an appropriate style.**

You see this announcement on an English-language website.

Articles wanted

A holiday to remember

Have you had a particularly good holiday? What was so special about it?

Who would you recommend this kind of holiday to and why?

Write an article answering these questions.

We will publish the best articles in our travel magazine next month.

Write your **article**.

Peer pressure

1a **Read the title and introduction to the article. What do you think the phrases a–d mean?**

a) follow the herd

b) the power of the pack

c) stand out from the crowd

d) do your own thing

1b **Discuss in your pairs.**

- Why do you think people follow the herd?
- Why do you think it can be difficult for people to stand out from the crowd?

2a **Read the first part of the article. Does it help to answer any of the questions in exercise 1b?**

The power of the pack

*Are you **following the herd**? It can be hard to **stand out from the crowd**, but understanding why will help you **do your own thing**!*

Raise your hand if you've ever shown up at a social event wearing the same trainers as your friends. Are there **traits** or behaviours – a hairstyle, the way you speak, the things you choose to eat – that **connect** you all? If one person starts following a **fad** diet, especially if it's been **raved about** in the media, the chances are everyone else will start doing it too. Why?

Psychologists have long studied how being part of a group –

whether that's your closest buddies or a crowd of strangers – influences your behaviour. They call this herd mentality, and while the way it guides your **preferences** for shoes and snacks may be harmless, understanding its role in bigger decisions can be a life-saving skill. Research shows, for example, that teenagers are more likely to take risks when they're part of a group. But even adults find it difficult to resist **peer pressure** for fear of seeming uncool, not only in what

they choose to wear or eat, but in the views and opinions they express. We tend to think of peer pressure as challenges your peers set you, but the most dangerous kind of peer pressure is the **influence** you don't really notice.

Humans are **social animals**, and much like sheep, we are driven to travel in packs. In ancient times, being part of the group gave us an evolutionary advantage: if you were a **loner**, you might fall behind and not survive an enemy attack. Imagine a **clique** of unfriendly guys at sports training as lions in the wild and you get the idea. You still feel safer if you surround yourself with like-minded people, no matter what your age.

2b **Look at the words in bold in the text in exercise 2a. Read the context carefully to work out what they mean. Then choose the correct words in the sentences below.**

a) My colleague is *raving about / connecting* this new song but I don't think it's anything special.

b) I enjoy my own company – I guess I've always been a bit of a *social animal / loner*.

c) Everyone has their own unique personality *preferences / traits*.

d) Your friends don't always have a positive *influence / pressure* on you.

e) There was a *clique / fad* of mean girls at my school. They weren't very friendly to anyone who wasn't in their group.

3a **Read the conclusion to the article and complete the sentences with the phrases in the box.**

be a good influence   be hard on yourself   be sure of yourself   do the right thing   face up to   get to you

So, what can you do to truly own your decisions without letting group pressure **(1)** ....?
The first step is to **(2)** .... the fact that herd mentality happens to everyone.
There's no need to be ashamed of worrying about what other people think. It can be difficult to
(3) .... and your opinions when everyone around you seems to think the
opposite, so don't **(4)** .... if you find it difficult to speak up. It takes courage to
voice what you truly believe, but once you do, you may well find that people are glad that you've
spoken out and may stand by you. And that's the power of the pack: it works both ways. When you
stand up and **(5)** .... , people will start to follow your example. In this way, you
can **(6)** .... on those around you!

3b **Discuss in your pairs. Do you agree with the advice given in the article?**

4 **Match the informal words and phrases (1–8) with the more formal equivalents (a–h).**

1 buddies
2 rave about
3 uncool
4 get to
5 loner
6 stand by
7 fad
8 show up

a) praise highly
b) a solitary person
c) support
d) friends
e) arrive
f) not fashionable
g) upset
h) trend

> **Vocabulary tip!**
>
> *A reflexive pronoun (e.g. yourself) is often used when the subject and the object of a clause are both the same, e.g.* You feel safer if **you** surround **yourself** with like-minded people.

✎ EXAM TASK: Writing (Part 2)

5 **Write your answer in 140–190 words in an appropriate style.**

You see this announcement in an English-language magazine.

> **Articles wanted**
>
> ## Standing out from the crowd
>
> Do you know someone who stands out from the crowd? What makes them stand out?
> How is this person a good example to others?
> Write us an article answering these questions.
> We'll publish the best ones in our magazine next month!

Write your **article**.

> **Exam tip!**
>
> *Be consistent with the register of your piece of writing. Don't mix very informal and formal language.*

Technophile or technophobe?

1a Match the words with the photos A–C.

> landline   manual camera   typewriter

1b Discuss the questions in pairs.

a) Which of these things did people use:

- to communicate with other people?

- to produce creative work?

b) What do people use instead of the items in the photos now?

2a Read the questions. Complete the definitions (a–c) with the words in bold. Then discuss the questions in pairs.

1 How many different electronic **devices** do you have?

2 How much time do you spend on your devices each day? Do you think you should spend more or less time using them?

3 Do you use all the **features** on your phone?

4 What electronic device or **gadget** would you like to get that you don't have at the moment? Why?

a) A .... is a small piece of equipment that does a useful job. It may be an item that is fun but not essential.

b) A .... is something that a machine offers or can do, e.g. long battery life, advanced camera, clear display.

c) A .... is a piece of computer hardware that has been designed for a particular purpose , e.g. mobile phone, tablet.

2b Discuss in your pairs. Which device do you spend most time using? What's so great about it? Use some of these phrases if you can.

> It's lightweight.
>
> It's the perfect size.
>
> It's easy to use.
>
> It's really cool.
>
> It's got tons of storage.
>
> It's got loads of apps.
>
> It looks great.

3a Which of the phrases in exercise 2b could you use to describe a website?

3b Look at the phrases in the box and discuss in pairs. Which phrases would you use to describe:

- a device?
- a website?

> clear menu system   easy to navigate   easily upgraded   high quality camera
> relevant content   useful links   user-friendly   visually appealing

4 **Think of a website which you use a lot and answer the questions. Discuss in your pairs.**

a) Which of the following words would you use to describe the website?

> contemporary   cutting-edge   engaging   fun   high-tech
>
> informative   innovative   professional   relevant   useful

b) Are there any negative points about the website? What are they?

5 **Look at the photos. Which person do you think is a technophile? Write three sentences to describe a technophile and three to describe a technophobe. Use the ideas in the box to help you.**

> cautious   (lack) confidence   confused   enthusiastic   followers   get left behind   keep up   latest
>
> linked   message   post status updates   social media   suspicious   tech-savvy   upgrade   upload pics

✏ EXAM TASK: Writing (Part 2)

6 **Write your answer in 140–190 words in an appropriate style.**

You see this announcement in an English-language magazine.

> ## Website reviews wanted
>
> Have you recently used a website you really liked? Write a review of the website, explaining what you like about it and what its most useful features are. Tell us who you would recommend this website to and why.
>
> The best reviews will be posted on our site!

Write your **review**.

Exam tip!

Remember to give reasons for any positive and negative review points.
The website's really useful **because it offers great advice on learning English**.
The menu isn't particularly helpful. **It doesn't take you to the right page!**

90 mins

Feel the beat!

1 **Discuss the questions in pairs.**

- Are you musical? Do you play an instrument or sing? If not, what would you like to be able to play?

- Are you in a band or would you like to be? Do you enjoy performing? Have you ever done a solo?

- How often do you go to gigs (concerts) or listen to music?

2 **Read the definitions and complete the words with the missing vowels.**

a) v _ c _ l _ s t   a person who sings, especially with a jazz band or pop group

b) l _ _ d   the main performer or part in a performance

c) s _ l _ _ s t   a musician who performs on their own

d) c h _ _ r   a group of people who sing together

e) c _ m p _ s _ r   a person who writes music

f) c _ n d _ c t _ r   a person who directs the performance of musicians

3a **Read what three people have to say about their music tastes. Complete the texts with the words in the box.**

artists   catchy   electric   headphones   keep in time   musical   in tune   tracks   tune in

I'd love to be able to dance, but I can't **(1)** .... , even though I listen to loads of music. I guess I missed out on the **(2)** .... gene the rest of my family seem to have! I love a **(3)** .... tune, though: anything I can sing along to when I'm driving. Just so long as no one else can hear me!

Jack

I play **(4)** .... guitar in a band and people are always really surprised when I tell them I love listening to the work of great composers, like Beethoven and Mozart. When I go to the cinema, I always **(5)** .... to the music in the background – the more dramatic, the better! I listen to music all the time but I can't sing – well, not **(6)** .... , anyway!

Zandra

You'll rarely find me without my **(7)** .... on. People often ask me what music I like, but as long as the **(8)** .... have skill, I'll listen to anything, even country or folk – which a lot of people my age aren't into – the words can be brilliant! I follow what's going on in the music business and I've always heard the latest **(9)** .... before anyone else.

Dan

3b Read the texts in exercise 3a again and answer the questions.

Which person:

keeps up to date with what's in the charts?   1 ....

appreciates the lyrics of songs?   2 ....

is into orchestral music?   3 ....

likes to sing in private?   4 ....

enjoys listening to film soundtracks?   5 ....

has no sense of rhythm?   6 ....

4 Match the words with the definitions. There are two definitions for each word.

- artistic (adj)   • arts (n)   • beat (n & v)

a) able to enjoy or create paintings, music, etc

b) hit repeatedly, e.g. a drum

c) the making, showing or performance of music, dance, drama or painting

d) the rhythm of a piece of music

e) showing skill and imagination

f) non-scientific subjects such as design, music and drama

5 Discuss in pairs. Which of the genres of music do you (not) listen to? Why? / Why not? Use some of the phrases in the box to describe your reaction to these kinds of music.

Useful language

It seems relaxing.   I can sing along.

It sounds horrible to me.   It gives me a boost.

It's not really my thing.   Don't you find it too loud?

It's fun and lively.   I find it really repetitive.

Exam tip!

Identify the different points you have to write about. Which three points do you need to write about in this exam task?

✎ **EXAM TASK: Writing (Part 2)**

6 Choose one of the items to write about in the exam task. Write your answer in 140–190 words in an appropriate style.

You see this announcement in an English-language music magazine.

Reviews wanted

Write us a review of *a gig / an album / a track you enjoy listening to* explaining what you like or liked about it, how it could be improved, and whether you would recommend it to a friend.

The best reviews will be published in our magazine next month!

Write your **review**.

Health goals

1 Discuss in pairs. Experts say the five health habits below make the biggest difference to a healthy lifestyle. Which of these do you (not) do? Which would you find hard to do? Why?

- Don't skip breakfast.
- Get 7 or 8 hours sleep.
- Do short bursts of exercise each day.

- Drink 8 glasses of water a day.
- Do 2 minutes of deep breathing every day.

2a Read the health goals of two students and the advice from lifestyle experts. Do you agree with the advice?

Joseph

HEALTH GOAL: Eat healthier. 'I make bad food choices when I'm in a hurry.'

EXPERT ADVICE: Joseph knows where he needs help, now he needs a specific goal to act on.

THE FIX: Plan ahead. When you have a plan, you're more likely to **stick to** it even when you're tired or hungry. Each day pack your bag with nuts, an apple and carrot sticks and make sure you eat every 3 to 5 hours to prevent hunger.

Ella

HEALTH GOAL: Exercise more. 'I'd like to jog instead of sleep in.'

EXPERT ADVICE: With no time frame, there's no urgency. Ella needs a measurable target to keep her motivated.

THE FIX: Print out a calendar and post it where you can see it. Then set yourself some achievable short-term goals, ie the ten days you want to wake up to jog this month, and a bigger long-term goal to keep you inspired, like **signing up** for a 5K race in the spring!

2b Discuss in your pairs. Explain your answers.

- Are you good at planning ahead or do you do things at the last minute? What sort of things do you plan ahead?
- What keeps you motivated in your studies or work?
- Has someone or something recently inspired you?

3 Read the emails. What change did each person make to their lifestyle? What was their motivation?

A

Thanks for your last email. Great to hear from you! You asked whether I've ever done anything for charity – well, yes, I have! I decided to **give up** eating chocolate for a month. I saw a programme on TV about diabetes and it really made me think. My friends and family supported me and helped me **get through** it. It wasn't easy cos I love sweet things but they helped by not eating cakes and stuff in front of me! **Cutting down on** sugary things not only made me feel physically better but mentally too – I feel like I can do anything if I put my mind to it! I find it easy to **do without** chocolate now. If I can do it, so can you!

B

How's it going? I said I'd let you know about my 5K race! Well, I did it! My cousin wanted to do a run to raise money for our local hospital. I wasn't sure it was such a good idea, but once I'd said yes, I felt like people were **counting on** me. It was really tough, especially when it was cold outside and I'd rather have been at home watching TV. So many times I felt like **backing out**! It was good to have my cousin to **talk** it **over** with and we kept each other going.

The atmosphere on the day was great! Everyone was **cheering** us **on** and I'll never forget how I felt when I crossed the line. I love running now and go several times a week. I know you said you weren't ready for a 5K run, but I really think you should **go for it**. You'll be **missing out** if you don't!

4 Look at the phrasal verbs in bold in exercises 2 and 3. Match each of the phrasal verbs with the definitions below.

1	cut down on	**a**	shout encouragement at	
2	give up	**b**	discuss	
3	do without	**c**	an expression used to encourage someone to do something	
4	stick to	**d**	depend on or trust	
5	count on	**e**	come to the end of a difficult experience	
6	back out	**f**	not have the chance to do something you might enjoy	
7	talk over	**g**	reduce	
8	miss out	**h**	decide not to do something you agreed to do	
9	cheer on	**i**	stop doing something	
10	sign up	**j**	continue doing something even if it's difficult	
11	go for it	**k**	manage not to have something	
12	get through	**l**	put your name on a list for something	

> **Vocabulary tip!**
>
> *Learn phrasal verbs in context. It's not always possible to guess the meaning from the words themselves. Reading and listening to the news is a great way to get familiar with phrasal verbs and how they are used.*

5 Are the emails in exercise 3 formal or informal? Tick the items in the lists which you could use to start and end an email to a friend.

To start

Hi there, Tom ☐

Dear Mr de Souza, ☐

To whom it may concern, ☐

Hey, Tom! ☐

Dear all, ☐

Hello. ☐

To end

Yours sincerely, ☐

Love, ☐

Best wishes, ☐

Regards, ☐

Cheers! ☐

Bye for now. ☐

✏ EXAM TASK: Writing (Part 2)

6 Write your answer in 140–190 words in an appropriate style.

You have received this email from your English-speaking friend, Kim.

Hi Ethan,

I've got important exams coming up next year and I think it's a good time to think about making some lifestyle changes and getting healthier. Can you give me any advice? I want to do something I know I can achieve! Do you think I should ask other people to do something with me?

Let me know what you think!

Thanks,

Kim

Write your **email.**

> **Exam tip!**
>
> *In an informal email you can use:*
> - *contractions, e.g.* don't, can't
> - *phrasal verbs, e.g.* put off *rather than* postpone
> - *colloquial language, e.g.* Awesome! Cool!

Fitness fanatics

1 Work in pairs. Choose the correct word for each definition in the sports knowledge quiz.

SPORTS QUIZ
are you a winner or a loser?

WHO AM I?

1 I try to prevent the other team from scoring goals.
2 I'm someone who competes against you in a game or competition.
3 I'm in charge of a football game and make certain the rules are followed.
4 I watch sports events rather than take part in them.

WHAT AM I?

5 I'm once round a race track.
6 I'm an advantage given to a team when someone in the other team breaks a rule.
7 I'm a place people go to do physical exercise and get fit.
8 I'm a prize which people win in sports competitions.

WHAT AM I LIKE?

9 I earn money from taking part in sport.
10 I'm strong and healthy and find sports easy.
11 I really want to win.
12 I enjoy sports.

athletic
penalty
competitive
professional
defender
gym   referee
spectator
lap
sporty
opponent
trophy

2 Circle the correct word(s) in the sentences.

a) *Professional / Amateur* athletes were originally not allowed to *represent / compete* in the Olympics as they were thought to have an advantage.

b) Unfortunately, our team *holds / makes* the record for losing the highest number of matches in a season!

c) Our team's in the *advantage / lead*! We're going to *win / qualify for* the championship!

d) A friend of mine *represented / played* his country in the games. He's very *proud / pleased* of his achievement!

e) We were *beaten / failed* in the semi-finals of the competition.

f) She has *put / set* a new world record with that incredible high jump!

3 Discuss the questions in pairs.

- Would you describe yourself as sporty?
- Do you think you are a competitive person?
- Do you work out at a gym? Why? / Why not?
- Do you think people who exercise are happier than those who don't?
- Do you think fitness posts on social media are a good idea?

4a Read the article about Marren's fitness experiences. Complete the text with the words in the box.

diet pills   fake   goal   healthily   impact   inadequate   lifting weights   lose   trainers   unrealistic

Seventeen-year-old Marren Miranti who lives near Houston, Texas, started going to the gym with her mum. Marren says she got into **(1)** .... and loved it. 'It's really satisfying to set a **(2)** .... , work hard and see your progress.' As Marren got more into fitness, she started following bodybuilders and personal **(3)** .... on social media, and it seemed harmless at first. She liked getting ideas for workouts and ways to eat **(4)** .... , but when she saw photos of people who were super-fit, it began to make her feel **(5)** .... 'If I'm not feeling very confident, seeing those photos can ruin my day.'

So what's the harm? 'The problem is that most of these posts aren't actually motivating us to be healthier,' explains Lexie Kite, co-director of Beauty Redefined, a not-for-profit organisation devoted to promoting positive body image online. 'They are motivating us to **(6)** .... weight and get fit to match up to certain beauty ideals – often at the expense of our health. These beauty ideals can lead to unhealthy behaviours like over-exercising or the use of **(7)** ....'

While some **(8)** .... photos are easy to spot, some posts are more subtle and even though we know these images aren't totally honest, they still have an **(9)** .... on us and may make us feel bad about our own bodies. Marren has become careful about who she follows. 'I like seeing a motivational message like "Keep working hard!"' says Marren. 'But I'm not interested in **(10)** .... goals. I'm proud of my body and me.'

4b Read the sentences containing phrases with *make* or *do*. Which of these ideas and opinions are mentioned in the text?

a) It doesn't **do you good** to spend too long in the gym.

b) **Make the most of** your gym sessions, and go as often as you can.

c) Some fitness posts **do more harm than good**.

d) Eating healthily **makes sense**, but diet pills are harmful.

e) Trying to keep up with beauty ideals can **make someone feel** inadequate.

f) Positive messages on social media help Marren to **do her best**.

g) Seeing photos of super-fit people **made a big difference** to Marren's confidence.

h) Marren realises her lack of self-esteem was often **to do with** seeing unrealistic role models.

> **Vocabulary tip!**
>
> Make *and* do *can often be confused. There are a number of common fixed expressions using these verbs.*

✏ EXAM TASK: Writing (Part 2)

5 Write your answer in 140–190 words in an appropriate style.

You have received this email from your English-speaking friend, Lee.

We've been talking about sport and fitness in our English class and I wanted to find out what my friends do to stay fit and feel good about themselves. Do you have any tips you could share about exercise? Do you think going to the gym is a good idea?

Let me know what you think!

Write your **email**.

> **Exam tip!**
>
> *You can improve your mark by checking your work when you have finished. Are your grammar and spelling accurate?*

What happened next?

1 **Read the sentences and look at the words in bold. Which of these do you do with:**

- your eyes?
- your mouth?
- your head?

a) I opened the curtains and **blinked** in surprise. It was spring, but the street was covered in snow!

b) Marta **chewed** the mouthful slowly. 'I think it needs a bit more salt,' she said.

c) Matt **gazed** into the baby's eyes. The baby looked back at him and smiled.

d) 'Quick! **Lick** your ice cream – it's melting in the sun.'

e) 'Can I borrow your car?' I asked May. She **shook** her head. 'Sorry, I need it this afternoon,' she said.

f) I **glanced** in the mirror and then stopped. My face was bright red!

g) Listen to Ryan **snoring**! No wonder no one else can get to sleep!

h) The woman **nodded** her head in agreement. 'Yes,' she said, 'I know exactly what you mean.'

i) The children **yawned**. 'I think it's time for bed!' said Grandad.

j) Joseph **stared** into the distance. He appeared to be deep in thought.

2 **Read the definitions and unscramble the sound words.**

a) c h _ _ _   You do this when your team wins the match.

b) s _ _ _   You do this when you are tired, sad or relieved.

c) s _ _   You do this when you cry.

d) c _ _   This is another word for 'shout'.

e) w h _ _ _ e r   You do this when you don't want someone to hear you.

f) g _ _ _   This is the sound you make when you're surprised.

g) g r _ _ _   You do this when you're asked to do something you don't want to do!

h) w h _ _ _ l e   This is a noise you make with your lips. You can make tunes this way.

> **Vocabulary tip!**
>
> *Find interesting synonyms for common words in order to enhance your writing, e.g.*
> shout: yell, howl, cry;
> interested: curious, absorbed, fascinated.

3a **Choose the correct option to complete the sentences.**

a) The man *crawled / kneeled* along the window ledge on his hands and knees. 'Don't fall!' cried his wife from below.

b) There was a bang in the kitchen. I *shivered / froze* on the spot. I'd thought I was alone in the house.

c) Andy woke up and *stretched / reached*. He'd had a great night's sleep for once.

d) The rollercoaster ride *dragged / rushed* along the track and I *gripped / squashed* the handrail, terrified.

e) The man *smashed / leaned* heavily against the wall and sighed with relief. He'd finally got away from the thieves.

f) They *wandered / dashed* through the park slowly, looking at the flowers.

g) Someone *tapped / stroked* at the window. 'Who's that at this time of night?' I wondered.

3b **Work in pairs. Choose the best answer: A or B.**

1 Which of these can you **kneel** on?   **A** a cushion   **B** a shelf

2 Which of these makes you **shiver**?   **A** being sleepy   **B** being cold

3 Which of these can you **reach** for?   **A** a light switch   **B** your ear

4 What could you **stroke**?   **A** a cat   **B** an ice cream

5 Which of these would you **drag**?   **A** a suitcase   **B** a feather

6 Which of these could you **squash**?   **A** a rock   **B** a piece of fruit

7 Which of these can you **smash**?   **A** a boot   **B** a glass

8 Why would you **dash**?   **A** you are late   **B** you are early

4a Complete the story with words in the box. You may need to change the form of the word.

> crash   freeze   grip   kneel   reach   shiver   stare   tap

It was a cold, dark night and the wind was **howling** down the chimney. I **(1)** .... and pulled the covers over me, grateful to be in my nice warm bed. Suddenly, someone **(2)** .... on my bedroom window. I nearly **jumped out of my skin**! Who was there? Why didn't they just **knock** at the door? I **(3)** .... for my torch on the bedside table. I crept out of bed, **(4)** .... the torch tightly.

I got hold of a corner of the curtain and **(5)** .... out into the night. There was no one there. Perhaps a leaf had blown against the window. Then I saw a shadow in the garden. There was someone there after all! I **(6)** .... with fear and my mouth went dry. Who was it? What did they want?

The figure was **(7)** .... on the path and started turning over plant pots. All of a sudden I **lost my temper**. I opened the window and **yelled** into the wind, 'I know you're there! What do you want?' I heard a pot **(8)** .... as the figure stood up, quickly. 'It's me!' came a voice. I **held my breath** and waited. 'I've lost my key and I thought you kept one under a plant pot. I knocked at the window but I didn't think you'd heard!' Of course! My cousin Shelly was staying the night and I'd forgotten all about it! 'I'll let you in!' I said, **going red**, and rushed to the door.

4b Discuss in your pairs. What do you like about this story?

4c Look at the words and phrases in bold in the story and answer the questions.

   a) Which words and phrases are sounds?

   b) Which ones are idioms?

   c) What do these words and phrases add to the story?

5a Look at these first lines from stories. What do you think happened next? Discuss your ideas in pairs.

- When I arrived at the station, my friend was already waiting on the platform.

- Leah turned to me and smiled sadly.

- It was half past four in the morning but Hiro was wide awake.

5b Choose one of the sentences and plan a story. Make notes.

 EXAM TASK: Writing (First for Schools, Part 2)

6 Write your answer in 140–190 words in an appropriate style.

Your English teacher has asked you to write a story for the school magazine.

Your story must begin with this sentence:

I could hear a noise in the distance.

Your story must include:

- a stranger

- a boat

Write your **story**.

Exam tip!

Use these features to make your story more interesting:

- *a range of tenses*

- *adjectives and adverbs*

- *direct speech*

- *idioms*

Ambition and betrayal

1a Work in pairs. Complete the genres with the missing vowels.

a) a d v e n t u r e

b) (_ _ t _) b _ _ g r _ p h y

c) c _ m _ d y

d) n _ n - f _ c t _ _ n

e) d r _ m _

f) s c _ _ n c _ f _ c t _ _ n

g) h _ s t _ r _ c _ l

h) h _ r r _ r

i) m y s t _ r y

j) c r _ m _

k) r _ m _ n c _

l) f _ n t _ s y

m) t h r _ l l _ r

1b Discuss the questions in your pairs.

• Which genres do you prefer in books and/or films?

• Do you like reading and watching the same genres? If not, why not?

• Are you an adventurous reader or film watcher? Or do you stick to your favourite genres?

2a Read the blurbs from books and films. Where do you find blurbs? What is the point of them?

A

Erin Kindling is no ordinary girl. She can see things which other people can't. Will she use her powers for good or for bad? The village of Little Inkling is about to find out …

B

Benedict and Marion are engaged to be married. There is only one obstacle: the rivalry of their families. Set during the war, this is a story of courage, willpower and enduring love.

C

Pedro and Mike are shipwrecked on a remote island. Cut off from the outside world, the two friends must face up to their fears and find their way home.

2b Read the blurbs again. Which genres do the books / films fit into? In which story (A, B or C) can you find each of the following themes?

bravery   despair   determination   evil   isolation   romance   the supernatural

3a Match the themes with the definitions.

1 ambition

2 betrayal

3 deception

4 discovery

5 freedom

6 jealousy

7 loneliness

8 survival

a) hiding the truth

b) being unhappy because someone has something you want

c) being able to do or say what you want

d) missing the company of other people

e) not being loyal to someone

f) continuing to exist in spite of difficult circumstances

g) finding something, especially for the first time

h) a strong feeling of wanting to be successful

3b **Complete the missing parts of speech.**

a) ambition (n) .... (adj)

b) betrayal (n) .... (v)

c) deception (n) .... (v)

.... (adj)

d) discovery (n) .... (v)

e) freedom (n) .... (v)

.... (adj)

f) jealousy (n) .... (adj)

g) loneliness (n) .... (adj)

h) survival (n) .... (v)

> **Vocabulary tip!**
>
> *When you learn a new word, find out other useful parts of speech too, for example:* loyal (adj), loyalty (n)

4 **Look at the images. Imagine a storyline for a book or film based on each image. What themes do the stories have?**

✏ EXAM TASK: Writing (First for Schools, Part 2)

5 **Write your answer in 140–190 words in an appropriate style.**

Answer the following question based on the set text.

You have been discussing the themes of the set text in your English class. Now your teacher has asked you to write this essay:

Describe one of the themes of the book. Why is it significant in the story? How does it affect the characters?

Write your **essay**.

> **Exam tip!**
>
> *Read the question very carefully and make sure you answer the question. Don't just write a ready-prepared answer!*

You've got style!

Marco

Amelia

George

Holly

1 Work in pairs. Look at the photos of the people and answer the questions.

a) Who is casually / smartly dressed?

b) Who is wearing designer gear?

c) Who is wearing a hood or shades?

d) What other items of clothing is each person wearing?

2a Read what three people say about their attitude to fashion. Who are you most similar to? Which of the people in exercise 1 do you think is speaking in each case?

I **live in** sports gear and rarely **get dressed up**. I don't wear skirts because I don't think they **suit** me – they just look wrong somehow. People sometimes say I look **scruffy** even when I've made an effort to look **elegant**! I do make silly mistakes, though, like wearing **odd** socks or having my jumper on **inside out**!

I dress for **comfort** rather than style. When you work outside like I do, you've got to wear things that are **practical** and suitable for outdoor work. I don't seem to have much **fashion sense**. I don't intend to be **unfashionable**, but I just don't know which clothes **go with** which!

I like to think I've got **style**. I try to follow the **latest trends**. I dress smartly most of the time, and I make sure everything **matches** – I'd never wear a black suit with brown shoes! Some people think I'm a bit **overdressed** at times, but it's important to look good – you never know who you might bump into!

2b Look at the words in bold in exercise 2a. What do they mean? Discuss in your pairs.

3 Complete the sentences with words from exercises 1 and 2. You may need to change the form of the word.

a) I look so .... ! My hair's a mess and there's a hole in my cardigan!

b) Do you think this tie .... this shirt, or is it too bright?

c) That colour really .... you. It's the same colour as your eyes.

d) I can't really afford .... , so I buy high street brands instead.

e) Jen's always been .... I don't think she pays any attention to trends.

f) You .... that jacket! I've never seen you wear anything else.

g) Can I borrow your .... ? It's really sunny outside and I can't find mine.

h) Don't you think you're a bit .... in that suit? We're only going to the shop!

i) Have I got my sweater on .... ? It doesn't feel right.

Vocabulary tip!

Use prefixes to make the opposites of adjectives.

comfort	→	**dis**comfort
practical	→	**im**practical
fashionable	→	**un**fashionable
overdressed	→	**under**dressed

PHOTOCOPIABLE

4   **Discuss the questions in pairs.**

- Have you ever worn a costume? What did you wear and why?

- Do you like to wear the same things as your friends? Why? / Why not?

- Whose dress sense do you admire? Why?

- Do you think you dress well?

- Is it important to you to be fashionable? Why?

5a   **Work in small groups. Look at photos A–D. These people are wearing less common items of clothing. Do you know what the items are called? If not, try to describe them using your own words and one of the phrases in the box.**

> **Useful language**
>
> *It's something you wear to …*
>
> *It's / They're made of …*
>
> *It's a kind of …*
>
> *It's / They're used for …*

5b   **Work in your groups. Find the words in photos A–D.**

> wig   helmet   buttons   kilt   bow tie
>
> formal dress   costume   biking gear
>
> braces   mask   gown   zip

> **Exam tip!**
>
> *Don't be afraid to ask the examiner to repeat the question.*
> I'm sorry, I didn't catch that.
> Could you say that again?
> Can you repeat that, please?

✎ EXAM TASK: Speaking (Part 1)

6   **Work in pairs. Take turns to ask and answer these questions.**

- What's your favourite item of clothing? Why?

- What kind of clothes do you like / dislike wearing and why?

- When do you dress smartly and when do you dress casually?

- Tell us about an outfit you particularly enjoy or have enjoyed wearing.

- Where do you get ideas for what to wear?

Mmm, that looks delicious!

1a **What are these items of food? Match the photos with the words.**

a) aubergine

b) cherries

c) leek

d) mint

e) nuts

f) pancakes

g) prawns

1b **Are these food items common where you come from? If so, what dishes are made with them? What foods are common in the diets of your country or region?**

2 **Work in pairs. Answer the food quiz. Compare your answers with another pair of students. Who got the most right?**

How well do you really know your food?

1 **Which of these foods can be salty?**
   a coffee   b nuts   c mint

2 **Indian curries can be hot or …**
   a mild   b weak   c tough

3 **Which of these foods can be either ripe or rotten?**
   a chocolate   b cherries   c rice

4 **Which of these foods is rich?**
   a cream   b mushrooms   c strawberries

5 **There's no flavour in this tea. It looks very …**
   a strong   b fresh   c weak

6 **Which of these foods can be tough?**
   a steak   b lentils   c spices

7 **Which of these is seafood?**
   a aubergine   b cheese   c prawns

8 **Which of these can be savoury or sweet?**
   a pancakes   b leek   c honey

3 **Read the article on pages 52 and 53. Which of these ways of eating appeals to you most? Why?**

Healthy secrets from around the world

It's a cliché: people in all corners of the world live on pizza, stuff down fries and drink cola by the litre. While it's true that **junk food** has penetrated the planet, when hunger strikes, people in other countries still open the fridge and find other <u>treats</u> to feast on – and some of their tastes are considerably healthier. Here's what a few of them say:

Remember how your parents always used to tell you to eat up your vegetables? Well, in France they're part of every meal, which often starts with salad or soup. They say vegetables are rich in **fibre** – which helps you feel full – they taste good too. It's also common to have three meals a day. If I'm really hungry, I'll have a snack like a sweet biscuit to keep me going, but I hardly ever have junk food. I think the variety means we have a pretty **well-balanced** diet.

A traditional Japanese bento box – which we have for lunch – has five colours of food in it, which means you're getting important **nutrients** from fruit, vegetables and whole grains. This helps power your system! People in Japan don't consume a lot of **dairy** products. That's important because they're difficult for humans to digest. We're encouraged to have a bite of everything – fussy eating is looked down on.

I live on **legumes**, like lentils and chickpeas. They're common in Indian food because they're a source of **protein** and have loads of B **vitamins** in them – great for keeping you energized! Many people in India are vegetarian. Half a cup of lentils has the protein of about 75g of meat and only one gram of **fat**. They're better for you than lamb or steak and keep you just as full.

4a Match the words from the text with their definitions. Are the words used as nouns or verbs in the text? Which of these words can be a noun and a verb?

1	bite	**a)**	the kind of things a person likes
2	consume	**b)**	something special
3	taste	**c)**	a small piece of food
4	treat	**d)**	eat or drink

4b Work in pairs. Discuss the meaning of the words in bold in the text. Use your dictionary to help you.

4c Work with another pair. Take turns to describe one of the words. Do your classmates know which word you are describing?

> **Vocabulary tip!**
>
> *Some nouns and verbs take the same form but they may be pronounced differently, e.g.*
> You should in**crease** the amount of fruit you eat each day.
> There's been an **in**crease in sales of fruit recently.

 EXAM TASK: Speaking (Part 1)

5 Work in pairs. Take turns to ask and answer these questions.

- What kind of food do you enjoy most? What don't you like? Why?
- Do you like food from other countries? What food do you like best?
- Do you like cooking? What kind of things do you cook?
- Tell me about a really good meal you've had. What was special about it?
- Who do you enjoy eating with? Why?
- Do you eat a balanced diet? What healthy food do you eat most often?
- How often do you go out for a meal? Where do you like going?

> **Exam tip!**
>
> *Say as much as you can in answer to the examiner's questions. It doesn't matter whether you answer yes or no!*
>
> Examiner: Do you like cooking?
>
> Student: No, not really. I don't have much time and I'm not very good at it!
>
> Student: Yes, I do! I like experimenting with recipes from around the world.

Training for success

1a Look at the professions in the box. Discuss in pairs. What do these people do?

> apprentice   coach   lecturer   student   teacher
> trainee   trainer   tutor

1b What is the verb for each of these nouns?

Example: *teacher (n) > teach (v)*

1c Which words can you add 'personal' in front of? How does it change the meaning?

2 Discuss in your pairs. Have you ever:

- studied something one-to-one?
  (What? Why? Did you like this way of learning?)

- studied for a non-academic qualification?
  (What? How do you use this skill?)

- taught someone to do something?
  (Who? What? Did you enjoy teaching?)

- given a lecture, talk or presentation?
  (Who to? What about? How did you feel?)

3a Look at the adjectives. Are these feelings positive or negative? Write P for Positive or N for Negative.

a) bad-tempered ....   **e)** depressed ....   **i)** irritated ....

b) bitter ....   **f)** fascinated ....   **j)** optimistic ....

c) concerned ....   **g)** furious ....   **k)** relieved ....

d) content ....   **h)** impatient ....   **l)** thrilled ....

3b Work in pairs. Choose an adjective. When was the last time you felt like this? Why? Tell your partner what happened.

4a Look at the two photos. How are they connected?

4b **How would you describe photo A in exercise 4a? Answer these questions.**

a) Who is in the photo?   **b)** Where are they?

c) What are they doing?   **d)** How do you think they are feeling?

5a **Write the words and phrases from the box in the correct column in the table. Which of the words and phrases are used to:**

- compare things (note similarities)?

- contrast things (note differences)?

- speculate about things (make guesses)?

> **Vocabulary tip!**
>
> *If you don't know an adjective, try to paraphrase it. She was **thrilled** to pass her test. / She was **really pleased** to pass her test.*

compare	contrast	speculate
too	*but*	*seem*

> appear to be   as well   both   but   however   look as if/as though   might/must/can't be   neither   on the other hand   perhaps   seem   whereas   while   though   too

5b **Now compare and contrast the two photos in exercise 4a. Use words and phrases from the exercises in this lesson.**

> **Exam tip!**
>
> *Describe the photos in as much detail as you can. It's fine to speculate about what the people are doing or how they are feeling, but don't talk about anything which isn't in the photos.*

EXAM TASK: Speaking (Part 2)

6a **Work in pairs. The photographs show people who are learning at work. Compare the photographs and say how important it is to be shown what to do in a new job.**

6b **Discuss in your pairs. Do you enjoy showing people what to do?**

Building blocks

1a **Complete the names for the metals by adding vowels.**

a) _ l _ m _ n _ _ m

b) t _ t _ n _ _ m

c) _ r _ n

d) c _ p p _ r

e) g _ l d

f) s _ l v _ r

1b **Look at the items commonly made from the metals in exercise 1a. Which metal is often used for each? Can you think of any other uses for the metals?**

> cans   jet planes   jewellery   pots and pans   wire

2a **What materials are used when constructing buildings? Match each definition with a material in the box.**

> brick   cement   glass   sand   steel   stone   tiles   wood

a) A small rectangular block used for building walls and houses.

b) This is found on beaches and in deserts and it is made from tiny pieces of rock.

c) A strong metal alloy which is made from iron.

d) A powder used to make concrete.

e) A hard, natural substance that is found in the ground.

f) A natural material which comes from trees.

g) This is hard and transparent and is used to make windows and bottles.

h) Pieces of hard-wearing material which are used to cover roofs, floors and walls.

2b **Discuss in pairs. How many of these materials can you see around you?**

3a **Work in your pairs. Group the list of words into two categories: materials and objects. Write M for material and O for object. Which words can go in both categories and what are their different meanings?**

blinds	carpet	diamond	photo	wardrobe ....
blanket	clay	duvet	plastic	wool ....
candle	cotton	fibreglass	rubber	
cardboard	curtains	lamp	straw	

3b **Answer the questions in your pairs.**

a) Look at the list of materials. Think of an item which is made from each of the materials.

b) Look at the list of objects. What material(s) is each object usually made from?

4a **What am I? Read the definitions and decide.**

a) I'm a kind of long tube. I'm hollow inside and water or gas flows through me.

b) I'm solid and heavy. I surround the flames which keep you warm. I'm often made from iron or stone.

c) I'm usually triangular in shape and covered in tiles. Without me, your home would get very wet!

d) I can be narrow or wide and you walk down me to get to different parts of a building.

e) I'm a metal box with a door. You put things inside me and I heat them up. I'm sometimes used to defrost frozen food.

f) I take smoke outside often through the roof of a building.

> **Vocabulary tip!**
>
> *If you don't know the word for something, describe it using words you **do** know.*
> *A: It's made of plastic and metal and has wires in it. You put it into the wall to make your TV work.*
> *B: Do you mean a plug?*
> *A: Yes, that's it!*

4b **Work in pairs. You may not know the words for the things in the photos. How can you describe them?**

 A
 B
 C
 D

> **Exam tip!**
>
> *Prepare for the photo task by choosing an interesting photo online. Talk about the photo for one minute. Practise with a friend and give each other feedback.*

✏ EXAM TASK: Speaking (Part 2)

5 **Work in pairs. The photographs show different kinds of home. Compare the photographs and say what the people might appreciate about living in each type of house.**

 A
 B

Park and ride

1 Look at the photos. Discuss the questions in pairs.

- Are all these means of public transport available where you live?

- Are there any other kinds of public transport people use in your town or city?

- How often do you use public transport?

- Which methods do you use? Which do you prefer? Why?

Vocabulary tip!

There are many everyday words which are different in British English and American English, e.g. underground, pavement, motorway *(UK);* subway, sidewalk, freeway *(US).*

2 Look at the words in the box. Which of these people operate vehicles? Which vehicles do they operate? Which of them does not operate a vehicle? How does this person get around?

> captain   chauffeur   courier   driver   motorist   pedestrian   pilot

3 Look at the words in the box and discuss the questions in your pairs.

> cancellations   cleanliness   comfort   delays   fares   privacy
> roadworks   routes   space   temperature   timetables   traffic jams

Which of these factors:

- can cause inconvenience when travelling by public transport?

- do you personally take into consideration when deciding whether to travel by public transport?

4a Read what two people think about public transport versus car use. Whose ideas are most similar to your own? Discuss in your pairs.

Some people say having a car gives you greater flexibility, but we all know the problems caused by driving. Using public transport can have its disadvantages. It's not always **reliable**, but it can often be more efficient – you can avoid **diversions** or getting **stuck** in jams.

Rising **fuel prices** and **maintenance** costs are causing people to think again about using their cars. High-speed trains will get you where you want to be in half the time and you can sit and relax. My car is more **convenient** if I need to **transport** a heavy item somewhere, but I limit my car use as much as I can.

4b **Use the words in bold from exercise 4a to complete the sentences.**

a) The bus I get to work is very .... I never have to wait more than ten minutes.

b) 'Sorry I'm late. There was a .... and I had to drive a long way round.'

c) The underground's cheap and .... There are stations close to home and work.

d) 'Hi, Jules. I'm .... in traffic! I'm going to be late for dinner. Sorry!'

e) .... are on the rise. It's very expensive to fill up these days.

f) I don't know much about car .... , apart from checking the tyres, oil and water.

g) They should use trains to .... goods rather than send them by road.

5a **Match the phrases with the definitions.**

> car share/carpool   park and ride   congestion charge   toll road

A
A facility where commuters and other people leave their cars in a designated car park and transfer to public transport for the rest of the journey.

B
A fee which drivers pay when they choose to drive into some city centres. The idea of the fee is to reduce the number of cars in the centre.

C
A system where people travelling to and from the same place each day travel together in order to save costs and reduce traffic on the roads.

D
A public highway which has a charge for using it. The money raised is used to cover building and maintenance costs.

5b **Discuss these questions in your pairs.**

- Are there any of the schemes from exercise 5a where you live? Do you think they're a good idea? Why? / Why not?

- How can governments increase the use of public transport in towns and cities?

Exam tip!

Read the question and options carefully. You can refer back to these if necessary during the task to make sure your discussion is relevant.

✎ EXAM TASK: Speaking (Part 3)

6 **Work in pairs. Imagine that a city wants to reduce congestion in the city centre. Here are some ideas being considered and a question for you to discuss.**

Look at the task and then talk to each other about how successful these ideas might be in a city.

charging for parking

Which of these ideas would be successful in reducing congestion in a city centre?

reducing public transport fares

investing in a new transport system

introducing a car share scheme

creating pedestrian-only zones

Catch some zzz!

1 **Discuss the questions in pairs.**

- Do you get enough sleep?
- Are you an 'early bird' or a 'night owl'? Does this affect how much sleep you have?
- How long does it take you to drop off?
- Do you ever oversleep?

2a **Can you complete the expressions about sleep?**

> in   catch   lose   beauty   log   wink   deep   fast

1 .... up on sleep

2 sleep like a ....

3 sleep ....

4 not sleep a ....

5 get your .... sleep

6 be in a .... sleep

7 .... sleep (over something)

8 be .... asleep

2b **Match the definitions with the expressions in exercise 2a. Three of the expressions have the same meaning.**

a) sleep later in the morning than usual

b) get no sleep

c) the sleep you need to look and feel good

d) sleep now because you didn't get enough sleep before

e) not get enough sleep because you are worried

f) sleep so well that nothing disturbs you

3a **Read what three people say about their sleep patterns. Who are you most similar to? Discuss in your pairs.**

I just can't fall asleep. To help myself **chill out**, I read on my iPad in bed but after that I lie there for ages. I start **stressing out**, counting how many hours there are til I have to get up again and thinking about how tired I'm going to be next day.

1 I don't have time to sleep! I get home around 7 and by the time I've eaten, checked my social media and started my college work, it's 10.00. I get to bed about midnight. I try not to **dwell on** problems but some nights it seems like I just **calm down** enough to get to sleep when the alarm goes off again!'

3 I wake up in the middle of the night, usually about 3 or 4 am. I know what time it is cos I check my phone. Then I start getting **worked up** about things – work, money, even stuff that doesn't usually get to me. Sometimes I don't go back to sleep cos I can't **switch off**.

3b **Look at the phrasal verbs in bold in exercise 3a. Which could you replace with *worry* or *worried*? Which could you replace with *relax*?**

> **Vocabulary tip!**
>
> *Phrasal verbs tend to be used in informal language, both in speaking and writing.*

4a Discuss in pairs. Decide which advice is most appropriate for each of the the speakers in exercise 3a. Which advice do you think *you* should follow?

A Looking at device screens revs your brain up and makes it harder to **unwind**. Make your bed a sanctuary – a sleep-only zone where screens are banned! Try listening to 'white noise'. The **calming** sound will tell you it's time to sleep.

B Keep a journal and spend about ten minutes each evening jotting down your **concerns**. This gives you time to reflect before you go to bed rather than in the middle of the night. If you do wake up, avoid looking at your phone – the glow from the screen will stimulate your brain and knowing how much (or how little) time you've got before getting up will only make you more **tense**.

C Make phone time a reward. Start your tasks directly and **treat yourself** to ten minutes of 'tech time' for every 50 minutes of work. Tell people you're constantly in touch with that you're going offline and ask them not to **contact** you until later.

4b Complete the sentence with the words in bold from A–C. You may have to change the form of the word.

a) Please stop .... me with updates! I'm trying to get to sleep!

b) It takes me a long time to .... after work. It's such a stressful job.

c) Archie's feeling quite .... at the moment because he's under a lot of pressure.

d) I'm going to .... to a massage to release the tension in my shoulders.

e) Have you got any .... about the new job or are you happy with the way it's going?

f) This music has a very .... effect on people. That's why we play it during beauty treatments.

✏️ **EXAM TASK: Speaking (Part 3)**

5a Work in pairs. Imagine that some classmates are concerned about getting enough sleep so that they can perform better at school. Here are some ideas and a question for you to discuss.

Look at the task and then talk to each other about which of these ideas would be most successful in helping students get more sleep. Talk together for about two minutes.

Exam tip!

Try to vary the language you use when you are speaking. For example, *use* delighted *or* thrilled *instead of* very happy.

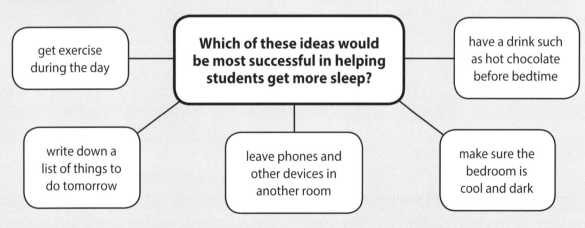

get exercise during the day

Which of these ideas would be most successful in helping students get more sleep?

have a drink such as hot chocolate before bedtime

write down a list of things to do tomorrow

leave phones and other devices in another room

make sure the bedroom is cool and dark

5b Discuss in your pairs which idea would be most successful. You have about one minute to decide.

A helping hand

1 Read Steff's blog about volunteering. Then match the paraphrases (a–f) with the phrases in bold in the text.

> **VB** ## Volunteering Blog
>
>
>
> I volunteered at a local 'clean up' day recently. There was an advert on our local website which said we should be proud of our town and asking for people to come along and help tidy up. They obviously **got** their message **across** because two hundred people turned up to help! We worked together in small groups on variety of different tasks. Our group **got on with** things like collecting rubbish, painting fences and clearing pathways. It was hard work, but once we **got down to** it, it felt great to be making a difference. My group **got along with** each other really well too and we had loads of fun.
>
> I recommend volunteering! You **get to** do something worthwhile for your community and make friends at the same time. It's easy to **get into** as well - just do a search for 'volunteering in my town' and you'll find loads of things you can do!

a) succeeded in communicating

b) made progress with

c) started putting effort into

d) be involved / interested in

e) have the chance to

f) had a good relationship with

2a Read the adverts for volunteers and answer the questions.

A ## Have you ever thought about volunteering?

Help older people in your community by visiting them and providing company, accompanying them to social events and doing small jobs, such as cleaning and shopping. We'll pair you with someone who has similar interests, whether it's movies, spending time outdoors or playing chess. All you need is a friendly personality and a willingness to get involved! **Call Ishani on 7775 4332 for further information.**

B ## LOVE SPORT? FANCY BECOMING A SPORTS VOLUNTEER?

We're looking for people of all ages to help out at the Berry Lane Sports Club. There are lots of things to get involved in, such as helping out at events, fund-raising and updating our webpage with recent photos and details about what's on. Come along to our open evening to find out more!

C ## CHARITY BOOKSHOP – VOLUNTEERS WANTED

We're looking for enthusiastic volunteers to help out at our bookshop for blind and visually impaired readers. We need people to help maintain our lending library, deal with enquiries from visitors to the shop and offer recommendations. You must be able to handle cash and preferably be a keen reader yourself! Call in to the shop and ask to speak to Jon.

In which volunteering role(s) would someone:

need to get along particularly well with elderly people? **1** ....

get to share an interest with someone else? **2** ....

get into if they want to share their knowledge with other people? **3** ....

need to get across information about forthcoming events? **4** ....

have to get on with a number of jobs including taking payment? **5** ....

2b Discuss in your pairs. Which of these volunteering roles would you find most interesting? Why?

3a **Find the phrases with *get* below. What do they mean?**

I'm trying to update our status on the webpage but I'm not getting anywhere. The internet connection's really slow.

Did you manage to get hold of the volunteers' coordinator? Her phone's been busy all morning.

I can't get over that programme about the orang-utan sanctuary in Borneo! It was amazing!

Can you get everyone's attention, please? We're about to announce the winners of the competition.

Vocabulary tip!

Get on (well) with *and* get along (well) with *are synonyms.* I've always **got on / got along** well **with** my sister.

3b **Complete the sentences with one of the phrases with *get* in this lesson.**

a) We're looking for volunteers who can .... people of all ages.

b) I don't think I'll .... travel to Kenya this summer.

c) Dad managed to .... the organiser to ask about volunteering on a farm in Ecuador.

d) The students could not .... how many homeless people there were in the city.

e) It's impossible to get everyone's .... when they're all talking so loudly.

f) Can you all please .... your work – there's a lot to do before we finish for the day.

g) I think I managed to .... how important the volunteers are to the organisation.

h) I'm not .... with my job applications. Maybe I need to update my CV.

Exam tip!

Get *is one of the most common verbs in English and is often used in informal expressions. Using informal language during the Speaking test is fine.*

✎ **EXAM TASK: Speaking (Part 3)**

4a **Work in pairs. Imagine a class of students wants to do some volunteering in their local community. Here are some ideas they're thinking about and a question for you to discuss.**

Look at the task and then talk to each other about why these ideas would be helpful to the local community. Talk together for about two minutes.

| tidying elderly people's gardens | **Why would these ideas be helpful to the local community?** | packing people's shopping in a supermarket |

visiting lonely people to chat

helping children with homework after school

walking dogs for an animal rescue centre

4b **Discuss in your pairs which idea would be most helpful to the local community. You have one minute.**

Home is where the heart is

1a Work in pairs and discuss the questions. Label the photo with the items in the list. Does your home have any of these? What things can you see in the house?

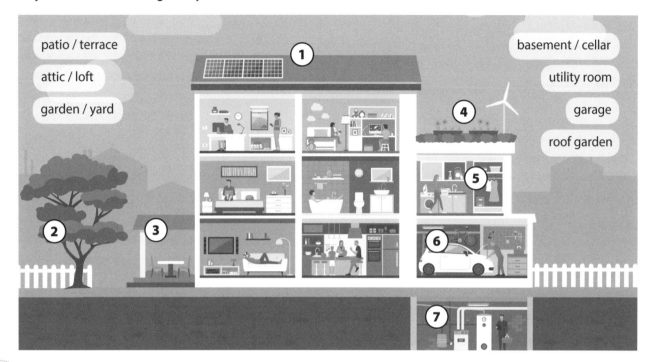

patio / terrace

attic / loft

garden / yard

basement / cellar

utility room

garage

roof garden

1b Look at the items in the list. How many of these can you see in the house? How useful are they? How common are these where you live?

air-conditioning   central heating   micro wind turbine   solar panels   sound system

1c Look at the items in the box and discuss the questions in your pairs.

a) Which of these things can you:

- sit on?
- put things in?
- put things on?

bench   counter   cupboard   hook   shed   stool

b) Where would you put these items in the house in exercise 1? Why?

2 What do you think is important in a home? Discuss these ideas in your pairs.

- amount of light
- decoration
- layout
- location
- atmosphere
- inhabitants
- level of comfort

3a Circle the correct option to complete the phrases.

a) I *feel / make* **at home** in this place. I'm always happy and calm here.

b) Please *be / make* **yourself at home**. Relax and do ask if you need anything.

c) I'm glad we're back from our holiday – **there's no** *home / place* **like home**!

d) I still think of home when I travel. After all, **home is where the** *head / heart* **is**!

e) This hotel is a **home from** *heart / home*. It's so comfortable and we've got everything we need.

3b Discuss the questions in pairs.

- Where do you feel most at home?
- How can you make someone feel at home when they visit you?
- Have you ever been anywhere you would call a home from home?
- What do you like about coming home after being away?

4 Choose the correct word in each sentence.

a) I live in a *three-storey* / *three-floor* house. My bedroom's up at the top.

b) I hate getting on and off *lifts* / *escalators*. They go round and round without stopping!

c) My office is on this floor at the end of the *path* / *corridor*. My name's on the door.

d) Sara lives in a quiet *residential* / *domestic* area of town.

e) There's a *construction* / *structure* site right across the road from my house. It's very noisy!

f) The university *headquarters* / *campus* is on top of a hill. The views are amazing.

g) Your cottage is in such an attractive *setting* / *venue*. You can look out over the fields.

h) They own a number of *properties* / *institutions* in the city which they rent out.

5 The adjectives in the box are all used to describe homes. Think of other things each of the adjectives can be used to describe.

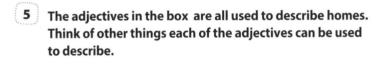

> comfortable   contemporary   cosy   luxurious
> spacious   stylish   traditional

Vocabulary tip!

When you learn adjectives, consider all the things they can describe. For example:
Your sister's very **attractive**.
I love this shop! The displays in the window are always so **attractive**.
By increasing the range of classes we can make the gym more **attractive** to members.

✏ EXAM TASK: Speaking (Part 4)

6 Work in pairs. Take it in turns to ask and answer the questions.

- What do you like best about where you live? (Why?)
- It is said that many people feel happiest when they're at home. Why do you think this is?
- What kind of homes do most people in your country live in?
- Who do you think are the best people to live with? (Why?)
- Is it important to have your own space at home? (Why?)
- Is it common for people to have pets in your country? What do you think about this?
- What kinds of things do people spend time doing at home where you live?

Exam tip!

Remember to respond to your partner's ideas and opinions. Try to say as much as possible but make sure your partner has a chance to speak too!

Festival fun

1 Read about three famous festivals. What do the festivals celebrate? Which festival does the photo show?

Holi

On the second day of this ancient religious festival, people throw coloured powder in bright shades, and dance and sing together. The festival has cultural significance for Hindus as they seek to end disagreements by forgiving and forgetting. It also marks the beginning of spring.

Harbin Ice Festival

This winter competition and festival takes place between December and the end of February each year and is a highlight for tourists. The cold nights in Harbin, a city in the north of China, are perfect for creating sculptures many metres high. Stunning light displays are created with the addition of sophisticated techniques.

Up Helly Aa

Held in the Shetland Islands in Scotland, this festival takes place on the last Tuesday of January every year. It is famous for its parades of people carrying fire torches and wearing Viking costumes and for the burning of a Viking boat at the end of the day. A historical festival which began in the 1800s, it celebrates the end of Christmas.

2 Circle the correct verbs to complete the sentences. Both verbs may be possible.

a) The highlight of Diwali for many is *decorating* / *creating* the home with candles and lights.

b) At Chinese New Year, amazing dragon dances are *performed* / *played* in cities across China.

c) During the Jewish festival of Purim, children *dress up in* / *put on* costumes to represent characters from a traditional story.

d) The Muslim festival of Eid al-Fitr *marks* / *celebrates* the end of Ramadan, the Islamic holy month.

e) Easter is a religious festival which is important in the Christian church. In many countries huge crowds *gather* / *attend* to watch parades.

f) We can learn a lot from historical festivals commemorating events that *took place* / *took part* in the past.

3 Discuss in your pairs. What other international festivals do you know about? When and where do they take place? What do they celebrate? Use these ideas to help you.

> religious occasions   historical events
>
> change of the seasons   agricultural holidays
>
> arts and music   food and drink   national holidays
>
> cultural events   royal holidays

Vocabulary tip!

Try to use a new word as soon as you have learned it. Then you will be more likely to remember it when you need it!

PHOTOCOPIABLE

4a Read what Sergi says about a local festival held in his town. Complete the sentences with the words in the box.

> celebration   custom   displays   is held   highlight   origin
> sculptures   traditional dress

I'm from the city of Valencia in Spain, where the festival of Las Fallas **(1)** .... every March. It's a traditional **(2)** .... which commemorates St Joseph, although the exact **(3)** .... of the festival is uncertain. The festival lasts five days, during which time you hear traditional music, see firework **(4)** .... , find people wearing **(5)** .... , and eat paella, a Spanish rice dish.

During the year, neighbourhood groups create amazing **(6)** .... from wood, paper and glue, which are then placed around the city. The biggest are constructed in the town hall square. The **(7)** .... is to set fire to the sculptures on the last night of the festival, known as La Cremà. Huge crowds gather to see them burn. It's the **(8)** .... of the year!

4b Discuss in your pairs. Are there any celebrations in your own country or town which are similar to Las Fallas?

5 Work in pairs. Describe an annual festival which takes place in your town, region or country and which your partner may not know about. Think about:

> origin   music and dance   food and drink   gifts
> clothes   family and friends   decorations   activities

Exam tip!

Use these phrases to give yourself a bit of thinking time:
That's an interesting question!
I've never thought about that before.
Let me see ...

✎ EXAM TASK: Speaking (Part 4)

6 Work in pairs. Take it in turns to ask and answer the questions.

- What do you think people enjoy about festivals?

- Why are festivals significant for a town, region or country?

- Do you think it is important for families to have their own traditions, such as celebrating birthdays together? Why? / Why not?

- In what way do you think preparing traditional food can bring people in a community closer?

- Do you think communities should continue to celebrate events which took place hundreds of years ago? Why? / Why not?

Fair trade

1 **Discuss these questions in pairs.**

- Do you hunt for bargains? Do you enjoy shopping in the sales?

- Do you look out for special offers such as 3 for 2 or Buy One Get One Free?

- How much time do you spend shopping per week?

- Is shopping more of a necessity or a leisure activity for you? Why?

- Do you like to buy fair trade or organic products?

2a **Read about three people's shopping habits. How are their ideas similar? How are they different?**

Adrian

I like to think of myself as an **ethical consumer**. So I buy **fair trade** products, which means workers or suppliers get a fair price for their **goods** and aren't **exploited**. Sometimes you have to spend a bit more, but that's fine with me. I'm not bothered about buying things which are **on offer**. I tend to avoid **big name brands** and **chains** because I'm in favour of supporting smaller independent businesses.

For me, buying **organic** is the only way to go. **Pesticides** and other chemicals create problems not only for wildlife but also for the plants they're meant to protect. Organic **produce** is more expensive because of **production costs** and a lack of **widespread demand**, but I think there are loads of health **benefits**. I also try to buy locally to keep my carbon footprint to a minimum, and because it's better for the local economy too.

Liv

Maya

I'll do anything to avoid going shopping! I'm into recycling and **upcycling** in a big way. It isn't just about making new things from old, but thinking about everything I consume. I make my own furniture from waste materials and I think about how I can re-use things like **packaging**. I even make my own cleaning products with **natural substances**. I'm **vegan** too, so I eat a plant-based diet. I grow some vegetables myself – and they taste much better!

2b **Which person:**

prefers purchasing goods produced with environmental benefits in mind?   **1** ....

would rather their money went to the area they live in?   **2** ....

makes sure that people producing the goods they buy are not disadvantaged?   **3** ....

considers every aspect of their lives when making consumer choices?   **4** ....

does not agree with eating or using animal products?   **5** ....

buys goods produced naturally despite higher prices?   **6** ....

PHOTOCOPIABLE

2c **Match the definitions with some of the words in bold in exercise 2a.**

a) not using artificial chemicals when keeping animals or growing food (adj)

b) to not pay or reward someone enough for something (v)

c) a number of similar shops and restaurants owned by the same company (n)

d) someone who does not eat meat, eggs, fish, milk or cheese (n)

e) a product that is made by a particular company (n)

f) food that is grown or made on a farm to be sold (n)

g) advantages (n)

h) a container or material that a product is sold in (n)

3a **Think about your own shopping habits and make a few notes. Consider:**

• how brand conscious you are

• how often, when and where you shop

• how bothered you are by environmental or ethical concerns

• whether your mood influences when you go shopping or what you buy

3b **Discuss your shopping habits in your pairs, using the phrases in the box to help you.**

Useful language

I think of myself as …	I try to …
If … , that's fine with me!	For me … is the only way to go.
I tend to …	I'm all for …
I'm in favour of …	I'm into … in a big way.

Vocabulary tip!

More informal words are often used in conversation and more formal ones in writing, but it depends on the situation. You might use more formal language in a job interview, and less formal language in an email to a friend.

4 **Match the pairs of synonyms.**

available (adj)   bargain (v)   bring out (v)   browse (v)

buy (v)   cheap (adj)   in stock (phr)   inexpensive (adj)

launch (v)   look around (v)   negotiate (v)   purchase (v)

✎ **EXAM TASK: Speaking (Part 4)**

5 **Work in pairs. Take it in turns to ask and answer the questions.**

• Do you think you have to spend a lot of money to get a good quality product?

• Why do you think some people enjoy shopping so much?

• Do you think advertising encourages people to buy more than they should? (Why? / Why not?)

• Do you think the way people shop will change in the future? (How?)

• How important is it for people to make ethical choices about what they buy?

Exam tip!

In this part of the Speaking test, don't be afraid to respond to or disagree with what your partner says.

Answers

Face to face (pages 6–7)

1a **Photo 1 (left):** make small talk (have a polite conversation with someone you don't know well)

Photo 2 (centre): overhear something (hear what someone is saying when they aren't talking to you)

Photo 3 (right): break the ice (make people feel comfortable when they've just met, often by starting a conversation)

2 **a)** hold **b)** making **c)** topic **d)** fascinating **e)** keeping **f)** deep **g)** endless

3b **a)** eavesdrop **b)** reveal **c)** interrupt

4 **a)** off **b)** down **c)** off **d)** up **e)** across **f)** out **g)** up

5 **1** C **2** B **3** A **4** D **5** C **6** A **7** D **8** B

Searching for solutions (pages 8–9)

1 **Photo 1 (left):** shows food leftovers (a half-eaten pizza).
Photo 2 (centre): shows unappealing vegetables ('ugly' carrots).
Photo 3 (right): shows a landfill site.
The common issue **all three photos** raise is food waste.

2a b

2b **a)** annually **b)** have led **c)** findings **d)** adds up to **e)** widespread **f)** adversely affects **g)** claim

3a **1** c) theory ('Research' or 'study' is done to find out more about a subject. A 'theory' is a set of ideas about a subject, e.g. *There are many different theories about how the brain works*.)

2 c) tips ('Information' and 'data' have a similar meaning; 'tips' are pieces of advice.)

3 a) effects ('Results' or 'findings' are information gathered from research; 'effects' are changes caused by an event or situation.)

4 c) propose ('Confirm' and 'prove' mean to show that something is true; 'propose' is a synonym for 'suggest'.)

5 a) deny (A person 'maintains' or 'claims' that something is true; 'deny' means to say something is not true, e.g. *He denied that he had met the woman before*.)

6 a) criticise ('Analyse' and 'examine' mean to study or think about something carefully; 'criticise' is to express disapproval of someone or something, e.g. *The inspector criticised the chef for wasting too much food*.)

7 c) comment ('Notice' means to realise something is happening, 'observe' means to notice as a result of watching or studying closely; 'comment' is to say or write an opinion about someone or something, e.g. *The customer commented that the chef's menu was unexciting*.)

3b **a)** criticised **b)** analysed **c)** claims / claimed **d)** theory **e)** proves **f)** recommendations

5a selling food close to its sell-by date; selling 'imperfect' produce

5b **a)** healthy / nutritious **b)** imperfect **c)** inexpensive **d)** surplus

6 **1** B **2** A **3** C **4** D **5** B **6** D **7** D **8** C

Flora and fauna (pages 10–11)

1 **a) amphibian:** toad **b) bird:** eagle, owl, swan **c) crustacean:** crab **d) insect:** beetle, wasp **e) mammal:** bat, bear, deer, fox, gorilla, leopard, seal, wolf **f) reptile:** chameleon, crocodile, python

2 **a)** domestic **b)** predators **c)** nocturnal **d)** species **e)** dominant

3a **1** a **2** instead, at **3** have, and **4** lots, them **5** can **6** which **7** is **8** their

3b **a)** instead (sentence 2) **b)** is (sentence 7) **c)** and (sentence 3) **d)** a = indefinite article (sentence 1) **e)** have (sentence 3) **Note:** 'have' can also be used as an auxiliary verb when used as part of a tense, e.g. *have taken, must have seen*. **f)** can (sentence 5) **g)** at (sentence 2) **h)** them (sentence 4) **i)** their (sentence 8) **j)** which (sentence 6) **Note:** 'that' is also possible. **k)** lots (sentence 4) **Note:** 'a lot' is also possible.

4a **a)** Animals typically associated with woodland or forest habitats: bat, bear, beetle, deer, fox, owl, toad, wasp, wolf **b)** Animals common in tropical rainforest habitats: chameleon, crocodile, gorilla, leopard, python

4b **1** flower **2** bud **3** stem **4** leaf **5** berry **6** seeds **7** roots

5 **1** and **2** which / that **3** of **4** only **5** their **6** there **7** it **8** in

Extreme conditions (pages 12–13)

1a **Photo 1 (left):** tornado
Photo 2 (centre): tsunami
Photo 3 (right): avalanche

2 **a)** volcanic (adjective), violently (adverb), gently (adverb)
b) majority (noun), seasonal (adjective)
c) powerful (adjective), remarkable(adjective)
d) obstruction (noun) **e)** dramatic (adjective), indication (noun) **f)** natural (adjective), movement (noun)
g) strengthen (verb), weaken (verb) **h)** downwards (adverb)

3a **a)** volcano **b)** violent **c)** gentle **d)** major **e)** season
f) power **g)** remark **h)** obstruct **i)** drama **j)** indicate
k) nature **l)** move **m)** strong **n)** weak **o)** down

3b **a)** volcano → volcanic (noun → adjective)
b) violent → violently (adjective → adverb)
c) gentle → gently (adjective → adverb)
d) major → majority (adjective → noun)
e) season → seasonal (noun → adjective)
f) power → powerful (noun → adjective)
g) remark → remarkable (noun/verb → adjective)
h) obstruct → obstruction (verb → noun)
i) drama → dramatic (noun → adjective)
j) indicate → indication (verb → noun)
k) nature → natural (noun → adjective)
l) move → movement (verb → noun)
m) strong → strengthen (adjective → verb)
n) weak → weaken (adjective → verb)
o) down → downwards (preposition → adverb)

4

adjective	adverb	noun	verb
-able	-ly	-ity	-en
-al	-wards	-ment	-ise / -ize
-ful		-tion	
-ic			

5a **1** noun **2** adjective **3** adverb **4** plural noun **5** noun
6 verb **7** adverb

5b **1** movement **2** significant **3** rapidly **4** skiers
5 destruction **6** notify **7** intentionally
Additional suffixes: -ant (adj), -er (n), -ify (v), -ally (adv)

6 **1** activity **2** forceful **3** unbelievable **4** coastal
5 dramatic **6** indication **7** damaging **8** destruction

Splash out or save up? (pages 14–15)

1a **a)** 3 **b)** 2 **c)** 1

1b **1** g **2** a **3** e **4** f **5** b **6** c **7** h **8** d

2 **a)** in **b)** up **c)** back **d)** on **e)** out **f)** off **g)** by

3a **a)** make **b)** make **c)** getting **d)** make **e)** make **f)** get

4 **1** investments **2** saving **3** irresponsible **4** earnings
5 economically **6** retirement **7** payments **8** banking

Making it big! (pages 16–17)

1a **A** comedian **B** novelist / author / writer
C camera operator **D** sound engineer

2a **1** camera operator: hopes to work on a Hollywood blockbuster

2 writer: hopes to write a bestselling novel

3 works in PR (a PR officer): would like to represent a major star

2b **a)** release **b)** cast **c)** screenwriting **d)** dialogue
e) promoting **f)** capture

3 **a)** (correct) **b)** appearances **c)** published **d)** (correct)
e) scene **f)** blockbuster

4 **Text 1 a) I'd like to make my name as** someone who …
b) I love … getting to work with members of the cast

Text 2 c) I doubt I'll go into screenwriting.
d) is something that **I personally find tough**.

Text 3 e) I often get asked what it is that I actually do.
f) I get **as much** publicity for them **as possible**

5b **1** best I had ever **2** are going to publish
3 was very fair **4** was entertained by

Disaster zone (pages 18–19)

1 **1** c **2** e **3** a **4** f **5** d **6** b

2 **a)** The problem was drought in South Africa. **b)** Kiara found a solution to help. **c)** Student's own answers.

3a **a)** She refused to be bothered by it. **b)** She thought it was important to understand the problem well.
c) She tried to find out about very absorbent materials which were natural.

3b Words or phrases to describe how people felt: *lose hope, discouraged*.

4 **a)** soak it up **b)** non-toxic **c)** declined **d)** effective
e) tackle

5 **1** b **2** c **3** a **4** d

6 **1** A **2** D **3** C

Going plastic-free (pages 20–21)

1 It shows a poster from the environmental organisation, Greenpeace, showing how a turtle can easily mistake a plastic bag for food / a jellyfish.

2b The writer supports banning or re-using plastic bags.

3 **1** though **2** When / As **3** While / Though **4** Unless
5 when / once / if **6** Once / When / If

4a **nouns:** impact, hazard, toxin, regulation, strategy, catastrophe; **verbs:** discard, accumulate, break down, contaminate, opt for, force to

4b **Paragraph 1:** build up / accumulate; danger / hazard; effect / impact, thrown away / discarded
Paragraph 2: decay / break down; pollute / contaminate; poisons / toxins; rules / regulations
Paragraph 3: choose / opt for; disaster / catastrophe; made to / forced to; plans / strategies

6 **a)** landfill (site) **b)** carbon footprint **c)** conscious
d) greenhouse gas **e)** harmful **f)** pesticide **g)** reusable
h) production

7a **1** E **2** B **3** D **4** A

Video game craze (pages 22–23)

1a The article is about electronic or video games; 'conquer the world' means 'be very successful'.

1b **a)** trend **b)** enthusiast **c)** object / aim **d)** fictional
e) innovative **f)** user **g)** launch **h)** brought out

2a **1** C **2** A **3** B

2b They are used to compare and contrast.

3 **a)** in comparison with **b)** significantly different
c) whereas **d)** far less **e)** not only **f)** Unlike

4 **4** G **5** E **6** D

Outside your comfort zone (pages 24–25)

1b **Suggested answers**

Positive feelings: thrilled, relaxed, cheerful, enthusiastic, determined

Negative feelings: uneasy, unsure, cautious, nervous, terrified

Synonyms: cautious: careful; **cheerful:** happy; **determined:** decisive; **enthusiastic:** eager, interested, keen, excited; **nervous:** anxious; **relaxed:** calm, easy-going; **terrified:** very frightened, very scared; **thrilled:** very pleased, delighted; **uneasy:** worried, concerned; **unsure:** uncertain

2a **1** comfort **2** felt **3** push **4** rush **5** drawn

2b **a)** bold: confident **b)** fascinating: really interesting
c) concerned: worried **d)** thrilling: exciting
e) amazing: brilliant

4 **1** E **2** B **3** A **4** C **5** D **6** E **7** A **8** C **9** E **10** B

In the workplace (pages 26–27)

1 **Photo 1 (left):** car dealer / car salesperson
Photo 2 (centre): construction workers
Photo 3 (right): shopkeeper / shop assistant

2a **1** d) Chief executive: An executive is someone employed by a business at a senior level. The Chief executive is the highest executive in a business and makes major decisions for the company. Also known as CEO (Chief Executive Officer).

2 g) firefighter: a firefighter puts out fires and educates the public about fire risk and safety

3 b) business analyst: someone who analyses an organisation or business and its systems and processes, usually to improve efficiency

4 c) civil servant: a person who works for the government, such as town council leaders or the armed forces

5 f) estate agent: someone who sells and rents out buildings and land for clients

6 a) sales rep: a person who sells products for a company ('rep' is short for 'representative')

7 e) lifeguard: someone who works at a swimming pool or beach and is responsible for saving anyone at risk of drowning

3a **1** C **2** A **3** B

3b **a)** shift work **b)** overtime **c)** income **d)** relationship
e) spreadsheet **f)** database **g)** deadline **h)** feedback
i) headquarters

3c **Text A** drawback: disadvantage
Text B payroll: a list of employees to be paid, specifying amount due to each
Text C backup: a copy of information held on a computer which is stored separately); desktop support: providing help for people who have problems with their PCs

4 **4** C **5** A **6** D **7** B **8** D **9** A **10** C

Culture club (pages 28–29)

1 **a)** customs and traditions **b)** beliefs **c)** dress
d) manners **e)** values **f)** arts **g)** food **h)** language
i) habits and behaviour

3 **a)** experimental, experimentally **b)** economical, economically **c)** historical, historically **d)** legal, legally
e) logical, logically **f)** natural, naturally **g)** occasional, occasionally

4 **1** c, culturally acceptable **2** g, cultural conflicts
3 h, cultural diversity **4** f, cultural stereotype
5 d, culture shock **6** a, cultural awareness **7** e, cultural misunderstanding **8** b, culturally significant

6 **Sample answer**

It's important for us to learn about other cultures because it helps us to avoid misunderstandings and disagreements.

There are many things which are common to everyone: we all eat, work and enjoy social events. However, the way people from other cultures do these things can be very different. Learning about another person's way of life is not only helpful, but also very interesting.

If you visit another country, it's important to be aware of traditions and how to behave in different situations. For example, it may not be acceptable to eat food with your left hand, or it could be rude to enter someone's house without removing your shoes. Of course, we all do things accidentally, but learning about the culture of the place we're visiting can mean we avoid such mistakes and help to improve relationships between people from different places.

People's beliefs and values can also vary widely and it's important to respect this. You may not follow the same religion as your neighbour, but accepting your differences will help you to get along.

In conclusion, making the effort to learn about other cultures helps to make the world a better place!

How well do you know yourself? (pages 30–31)

1a **1** Eagle **2** Parrot

1b **Eagle:** self-assured (confident), fearless (not afraid of anything), clear (easy to understand) and confident (sure of yourself), **Parrot:** chatty (talkative), fun (entertaining), lucky (fortunate), easy (not difficult), spontaneous (doing things without planning them first)

2 **a)** bossy **b)** calm **c)** careful **d)** caring / kind / thoughtful **e)** thorough **f)** easy-going **g)** helpful / kind

3b Merrick uses 'chameleon' to mean someone who can adapt to different social situations.

4a **a)** supportive **b)** indecisive **c)** imaginative **d)** bold **e)** cautious **f)** impatient **g)** considerate **h)** rational **i)** sociable **j)** energetic

4b **a)** unsupportive **b)** decisive **c)** unimaginative **f)** patient **g)** inconsiderate **h)** irrational **i)** unsociable

bold, cautious and *energetic* don't take prefixes.

Suggested answers (opposite adjectives):

bold: unadventurous, cautious; **cautious:** bold, brave, careless; **energetic:** lazy, tired

5 **Sample answer**

Friends and family have different roles in our lives, so it isn't possible to say that one is more important than the other in my opinion.

Often in a family there are people who are like each other, but this isn't always the case. They say you can choose your friends but you can't choose your family, and I think one of the ways in which we *do* choose our friends is that we have similar personalities. I'm impatient, decisive and competitive and many of my friends are too. However, my best friend complements my personality because she's patient and considerate – we make a great team!

When you're dealing with problems, the first people many of us talk to are family because they're supportive and you can count on them not to talk about your problems outside the family.

Friends are also important because we spend lots of free time with them and share similar interests and hobbies which people in our families may not.

In summary, neither friends nor family are more important and who we spend time with depends completely on the situation.

Setting off (pages 32–33)

1a **a)** board a plane **b)** call a taxi **c)** check in / collect your luggage **d)** make an online booking **e)** download / collect a boarding pass / an e-ticket **f)** check in / arrive at the airport **g)** pack / collect / check in a suitcase **h)** arrive at your destination **i)** go through passport control / customs / security

1b **Suggested answers**
Photo 1: making an online booking
Photo 2: going through security
Photo 3: boarding a plane
Photo 4: arriving at his destination

At the airport passengers also need to check in. Once they have arrived at their destination they get off the plane or disembark, collect their luggage and go through customs or passport control. They might call a taxi from the airport.

2a board (get on); collect (pick up)

2b **a)** pulled (her) over **b)** pulled up **c)** pulled out

3 **1** away **2** off **3** in **4** up **5** around **6** back **7** to **8** out / off **9** off **10** up **11** off / over **12** in **13** off **14** off

4 **a)** turn up **b)** get in **c)** sees / saw (me) off **d)** dropped (us) off **e)** stopping off / over **f)** setting off / out **g)** looking forward to **h)** look around

6 Sample answer

The best way to travel is not necessarily the way that gets you there the quickest. There are other factors to take into consideration too.

Flying is the form of transport that most people would say is the fastest. While planes can cover thousands of kilometres quickly, checking in, getting through airport security and collecting luggage all takes time and can be stressful, especially when the airport is busy. On the other hand, train travel is much more comfortable and doesn't require checking in. Although it takes longer, you can sit back and look out of the window, arriving much more refreshed.

The length of journey you make has an impact on the form of transport you choose. If you're travelling from Europe to Australia, the easiest way to do it is by air. But for shorter journeys, driving is very convenient.

For some people, cost can also be a consideration: they may have to take cheaper forms. Travelling by bus is usually an economical option.

For me, the best way to travel is the one that you enjoy the most and is the most relaxing.

Getting away from it all (pages 34–35)

1 an advertisement for a holiday company

2 **1** c **2** f **3** a **4** b **5** d **6** e

3a **1** beach holiday **2** backpacking **3** safari **4** spa break **5** city break **6** ecotourism **7** cruise

4a Students were asked to write about a holiday they would like to go on (and why), what they would like to do there, and who they would like to travel with (and why).

4b **a)** excursions **b)** touristy **c)** an itinerary **d)** going away **e)** stunning scenery **f)** going on a tour

6 Sample answer

The best holiday I have ever had was when I went to Hawaii and went on a diving excursion on the coral reefs. I'd never been diving before and felt a little nervous, but I knew it would definitely be worth it.

Below the surface was a whole new world, with amazing creatures and corals, all in beautiful colours in the bright blue ocean. It was quiet and peaceful there too and I captured some amazing shots with an underwater camera. It was stunning!

It is very important that visitors to the area are aware of environmental problems on the reefs. Parts of the reef are slowly being killed off and this is in part caused by tourism.

I would definitely recommend a a scuba diving trip to people who are prepared to be responsible and follow the instructions they are given. It's the experience of a lifetime!

Peer pressure (pages 36–37)

1a **a)** follow the herd or follow the crowd: to do what most other people are doing (animals like buffalo move in herds)

b) the ability of a group of people to affect the actions and beliefs of others (animals like wolves hunt in packs)

c) be clearly better or noticeably different from others

d) do what you want without worrying what anyone else thinks

2b **a)** raving about **b)** loner **c)** traits **d)** influence **e)** clique

3a **1** get to you **2** face up to **3** be sure of yourself **4** be hard on yourself **5** do the right thing **6** be a good influence

4 **1** d **2** a **3** f **4** g **5** b **6** c **7** h **8** e

5 Sample answer

Everyone knows someone who stands out from the crowd. It may be someone who's very good at something, such as sport or art, or it could be someone who has a lively personality and makes friends very easily.

For me, my sister Joella is someone who stands out. She is one of the kindest and most caring people I know. She is always there when I need someone to talk to. When I have issues at work or with a friend, Joella is the first person I go to for advice.

Although she's a fairly quiet person, Joella also stands up for what she believes in. She isn't afraid to express her opinions and she is someone who people take seriously. She is firm but calm and in this way she has a good influence on those around her. She works hard, respects other people and follows her dreams. For me, Joella is a great example of how someone can be quiet, but still stand out from the crowd.

Technophile or technophobe? (pages 38–39)

1a **A** manual camera **B** typewriter **C** landline

1b **a)** communicate: landline; produce creative work: typewriter, manual camera

b) **A** mobile phone / digital camera **B** computer / laptop / tablet **C** mobile (phone)

2a **a)** gadget **b)** feature **c)** device

3a It looks great. It's easy to use. It's really cool.

3b **devices:** user-friendly, visually appealing, easy to navigate, clear menu system, high-quality camera, easily upgraded; **website:** user-friendly, visually appealing, easy to navigate, relevant content, clear menu system, useful links

5 A technophile is someone who loves technology. A technophobe is someone who dislikes it.

6 **Sample answer**

I've been using a website called 'Gadgets' recently, which is a brilliant place to find out about the latest electronic devices. What makes it so useful is that all the information is in the form of reviews by people who've already got a particular device. It's perfect if you're considering upgrading your phone.

The website is really informative and it's user-friendly because it's easy to navigate and the information provided is really honest. The website's got a few fun and engaging features too: you can chat to people who've bought products and even try out some of them virtually!

I would recommend this website to anyone who isn't particularly tech-savvy. It's easy to access and has up-to-date, relevant content, which helps you make important decisions about what to buy.

Feel the beat! (pages 40–41)

2 **a)** vocalist **b)** lead **c)** soloist **d)** choir **e)** composer **f)** conductor

3a **1** keep in time **2** musical **3** catchy **4** electric **5** tune in **6** in tune **7** headphones **8** artists **9** tracks

3b **a)** Dan **b)** Dan **c)** Zandra **d)** Jack **e)** Zandra **f)** Jack

4 **a)** & **e)** artistic **b)** & **d)** beat **c)** & **f)** arts

6 **Sample answer**

I went to see a band called Generation Z play at the Arena last night. It was one of the best gigs I've ever been to. The lead singer's got an incredible voice and the guitarist did a really amazing solo in one of the songs. They're a really talented band and they're not only great musicians but also write some brilliant lyrics. Some songs are funny and others are more serious, but the words make you think. A lot of their music is very catchy, so everyone danced along, even me, and I don't usually have a good sense of rhythm!

I don't think the band themselves could be any better, though the venue was quite small and crowded, so it got a bit hot and there wasn't a lot of space to dance.

I'd definitely recommend going to this gig. The artists are really great live, and even if guitar bands aren't your thing, you'll definitely appreciate their musical skill.

Health goals (pages 42–43)

3 A reduced the amount of sugar they ate / gave up chocolate for a month. B did a 5K run.

A's motivation was seeing a TV programme about diabetes. B was encouraged by a cousin who wanted to raise money for the local hospital.

4 **1** g **2** i **3** k **4** j **5** d **6** h **7** b **8** f **9** a **10** l **11** c **12** e

5 They are informal emails.

To start: Hi there, Tom; Hey, Tom! Hello.
To end: Love, Cheers! Bye for now!

6 **Sample answer**

Hi Kim!

Great to hear from you! Getting healthier will definitely help you cope with your exams next year. My top advice would be to get more sleep. I used to get around five hours. I kept waking up to check my phone! Now I've started leaving my phone in the kitchen at night. I get about seven or eight hours now and I feel so much better for it!

Doing something with other people sounds like a cool idea. It's good to have other people to encourage you. What about doing something for charity? You could get fit and raise money at the same time. Maybe doing a 5K run or even something like a bungee jump because you need to train for that too. But you don't want to do anything too scary or you might end up backing out!

If you're trying out a new exercise routine, it's best to give yourself a realistic target first. Do small amounts first, even if it's only ten minutes a day, and then build up.

Good luck with whatever you decide to do and let me know how it goes!

Ethan x

Fitness fanatics (pages 44–45)

1 **1** defender **2** opponent **3** referee **4** spectator **5** lap **6** penalty **7** gym **8** trophy **9** professional **10** athletic **11** competitive **12** sporty

2 **a)** Professional, compete **b)** holds **c)** lead, qualify **d)** represented, proud **e)** beaten **f)** set

4a **1** lifting weights **2** goal **3** trainers **4** healthily **5** inadequate **6** lose **7** diet pills **8** fake **9** impact **10** unrealistic

4b All of these ideas and opinions are expressed in the text, except for b and d.

a 'unhealthy behaviours like over-exercising'

c 'They are motivating us to lose weight and get fit to match up to certain beauty ideals – often at the expense of our health.'

e 'they still have an **impact** on us and may make us feel bad about our own bodies.'

f 'I like seeing a motivational message like "Keep working hard!"' says Marren.

g 'If I'm not feeling very confident, seeing those photos can ruin my day.'

h 'when she saw photos of people who were super-fit, it began to make her feel inadequate'

5 **Sample answer**

Hi Lee

Thanks for your email. Keeping fit and being healthy are really important for me. I play football every weekend with my friends. I can't imagine not doing some kind of exercise. Feeling good about yourself and spending time with your mates is what it's all about. It's good for your confidence and your self-esteem. I broke my ankle a few years ago and I wasn't able to play. That was one of the worst times. I just felt so down.

Going to the gym is definitely a good thing to do. I go three times a week before work. But you don't want to overdo it. I do look at fitness websites to get ideas about healthy eating and what kind of workouts to do. But any posts which suggest you should cut out food groups or spend hours in the gym are probably fake. They just lead to unrealistic expectations. I think you can make a big difference to the way you look and feel just by doing regular exercise and eating well.

I hope that answers your questions!

Jay ☺

What happened next? (pages 46–47)

1 **eyes:** blink, gaze, glance, stare
mouth: chew, lick, snore, yawn
head: shake, nod

2 **a)** cheer **b)** sigh **c)** sob **d)** cry **e)** whisper **f)** gasp **g)** groan **h)** whistle

3a **a)** crawled **b)** froze **c)** stretched **d)** rushed, gripped **e)** leaned **f)** wandered **g)** tapped

3b **1** A **2** B **3** A **4** A **5** A **6** B **7** B **8** A

4a **1** shivered **2** tapped **3** reached **4** gripping **5** stared **6** froze **7** kneeling **8** crash

4c **a)** knock, yell, howl

b) jump out of your skin, lose your temper, hold your breath, go red

c) They make the story more interesting and sound more natural.

6 **Sample answer**

I could hear a noise in the distance. It sounded like someone was tapping. I glanced around but there was no one in the street. The noise seemed to be coming from the direction of the harbour, so I wandered along to find out what it was.

As I came round the corner into the harbour, I gasped in surprise. Floating in front of me was a boat made of wood and paper! A small group of people were busy finishing it. As I stood staring, a man I'd never seen before walked up to me.

'Amazing, isn't it?' he said.

'Yes, but what it's for?' I asked. 'Why are you making a boat from paper?'

'It's for the Sailor's Festival this evening,' he replied. 'We burn the boat in memory of sailors everywhere.' Then he walked away, whistling cheerfully.

As night fell, I stood amongst the crowds and watched the flames. Everyone cheered as fireworks filled the sky. 'What a lovely celebration!' I thought as I walked thoughtfully back home.

Ambition and betrayal (pages 48–49)

1a **a)** adventure **b)** (auto)-biography **c)** comedy **d)** non-fiction **e)** drama **f)** science fiction **g)** historical **h)** horror **i)** mystery **j)** crime **k)** romance **l)** fantasy **m)** thriller

2a Blurbs are on the back cover of a book, on DVD cases, in catalogues and on websites. A blurb is a short description of a book or film, used for promotion. It often includes quotes from published reviews.

2b **Genres:** **A** mystery / fantasy **B** romance / historical **C** action / adventure

Themes: **A** the supernatural, evil **B** bravery, determination, romance **C** isolation, despair

3a **1** h **2** e **3** a **4** g **5** c **6** b **7** d **8** f

3b **a)** ambitious (adj) **b)** betray (v) **c)** deceive (v), deceptive (adj) **d)** discover (v) **e)** free (v), free (adj) **f)** jealous **g)** lonely (adj) **h)** survive (v)

You've got style! (pages 50–51)

1 **a)** Holly and George are casually-dressed; Marco and Amelia are smartly dressed. **b)** Marco is wearing designer gear. **c)** Holly has a hood; Marco is wearing shades. **d)** Marco is wearing a jacket and polo neck top; George is wearing overalls and a hard hat; Amelia is wearing a suit; Holly is wearing a (woolly) hat and a hoodie (hooded jacket).

2a **Suggested answers**

a) Holly   b) George   c) Marco or Amelia

2b **I live in sports gear:** I always wear sports clothes; **get dressed up:** wear smart or special clothes; **suit someone:** look good on someone; **scruffy:** messy; **elegant:** smart and attractive; **odd socks:** socks which don't match (not a pair); **inside out:** with the seams and label on the outside; **comfort:** feeling relaxed and comfortable; **practical:** useful or suitable for a particular purpose; **fashion sense:** knowing what's in fashion; **unfashionable:** not popular at the current time; **go with / match:** look good together; **style:** looking attractive and fashionable; **latest trends:** what people are wearing right now; **overdressed:** dressed in clothes that are too formal for the situation

3 **a)** scruffy **b)** goes with / matches **c)** suits **d)** designer gear **e)** unfashionable **f)** live in **g)** shades **h)** overdressed **i)** inside out

5b wig D, helmet B, buttons A and C, kilt A, bow tie C, formal dress C, biking gear B, braces C, mask D, gown D, zip B

Mmm, that looks delicious! (pages 52–53)

1a **1** f **2** a **3** g **4** d **5** e **6** b **7** c

2a **1** b **2** a **3** b **4** a **5** c **6** a **7** c **8** a

4a **1** c **2** d **3** a **4** b

taste, *bite* and *treat* can all be used as nouns or verbs

4b **fibre:** parts of plants that you eat but can't digest – fibre helps to move food through your body
well-balanced: contains all the different food groups you need to keep you healthy
nutrients: substances which are necessary for animals and plants to live and grow
dairy: containing milk
legumes: food such as beans and peas
protein: natural substance that is found in food such as fish, meat, eggs and cheese
vitamins: natural chemicals in food that we need for good health
fat: an oily substance found in some foods

Training for success (pages 54–55)

1a An **apprentice** is someone who learns a trade from an expert or company: they don't usually get paid much during their training period.

A **coach** usually teaches sport. A life coach gives advice on lifestyle choices.

A **lecturer** teaches students at college or university.

A **student** is a person or child who is learning at school, college or university. It can also be used to refer to someone who is spending time learning about a subject they are interested in.

A **teacher** gives lessons in a school.

A **trainer** is someone who teaches someone a particular skill, often at work or in sport. The person who is learning this skill at work is the **trainee**.

A **tutor** usually works in a British college or university, or gives lessons to small groups or individuals outside of school or college, such as music tuition or extra maths lessons.

1b **apprentice** (n) > be an apprentice / be apprenticed to (v)
coach (n) > coach (someone or a team) (v)
lecture (n) > lecture / give lectures (v)
student (n) > study (v)
teacher (n) > teach (v)
trainer (n) > train (someone) to do (something) / give (someone) training in (something) (v)
trainee (n) > train to do something / train as (a profession) (v)
tutor (n) > tutor (v)

3a **positive feelings:** content, fascinated, optimistic, relieved, thrilled;
negative feelings: bad-tempered, bitter, concerned, depressed, furious, impatient, irritated

4a Both photos show people who have taken exams or tests.

4b **Suggested answers**

a) There are several high school or college students in the photo.

b) It looks as if they are at school or college.

c) It looks like they have just received their exam results and they are congratulating each other.

d) I think these students have passed their exams and are feeling relieved and thrilled.

5a **compare:** too, both, neither, as well
contrast: but, whereas, while, though, however, on the other hand
speculate: seem, appear to be, look as if / as though, might / must / can't be, perhaps

5b **Suggested answer**

Both photos show students who have finished exams or tests. The students in the first photo are at school or college and it looks as if they have just received their exam results. They must have passed because they are smiling and congratulating each other. The girl in the second photo has just taken her driving test, but it looks as though she has failed because she has her head in her hands and the driving instructor looks very serious. The students in the first photo look relieved and thrilled, whereas the girl in the photo on the right looks sad. Perhaps she is feeling depressed.

Building blocks (pages 56–57)

1a **a)** aluminium **b)** titanium **c)** iron **d)** copper **e)** gold **f)** silver

1b **drinks cans:** aluminium; **jet planes:** aluminium, titanium; **jewellery:** gold and silver; **pots and pans:** iron, copper; **wire:** copper

Suggested answers

aluminium: aluminium foil, car parts; **titanium:** spacecraft, water-resistant watches; **iron:** car parts, most iron is used to make steel (an alloy); **copper:** pipes; **gold:** precious items, medals; **silver:** medals, batteries, cutlery;

2a **a)** brick **b)** sand **c)** steel **d)** cement **e)** stone **f)** wood **g)** glass **h)** tiles

3a blinds (O), blanket (O), candle (O), cardboard (M), carpet (O), clay (M), cotton (M), curtains (O), diamond (O/M) (A diamond is a precious stone which is also sometimes used as a material), duvet (O), fibreglass (M), lamp (O), photo (O), plastic (M), rubber (M/O) (Rubber is made from a sticky substance collected from the trunk of a rubber tree. A rubber is an eraser in British English; in US English a rubber is an informal word for a condom), straw (M/O) (straw is a material made from the dried stalks of crops such as wheat or barley. A straw is a thin tube of paper or plastic used for drinking.), wardrobe (O), wool (M).

3b **a) Suggested answers**

cardboard: boxes, cartons, packages; **clay:** plates, vases, decorative items; **cotton:** shirts, skirts, sheets; **diamond:** machine parts, engagement rings and other jewellery; **fibreglass:** boats, bathtubs, surfboards,

swimming pools; **plastic:** bottles, packaging, cups, buckets, toys; **rubber:** tyres, gloves, erasers, wellington boots; **straw:** hats, bedding for animals, used as a building material when mixed with clay; **wool:** sweaters, gloves, hats, scarves

b) Suggested answers

blinds: wood, plastic, metal; **a blanket:** wool, synthetic fibres; **a candle:** wax; **a carpet:** synthetic fibres, wool; **curtains:** fabric, e.g. cotton, silk; **a duvet:** cotton, feathers, foam; **a lamp:** fabric, metal, wires, glass (bulb); **a photo:** paper, ink; **a straw:** paper, plastic; **a rubber:** rubber, latex; **a wardrobe:** wood, metal

4a **a)** a pipe **b)** a fireplace **c)** a roof **d)** a corridor / a hallway **e)** a microwave oven **f)** a chimney

4b **Suggested answers**

A It's big and strong. It's usually made of wood. It supports the roof of your house. (a beam)

B It's a room at the top of the house, under the roof. It's sometimes used for storing things you don't use very much. (an attic)

C It's outside the house. It's usually made of concrete. You can sit here when it's sunny. (a patio or terrace)

D It's a kind of window which you have in the roof of a house. (a skylight)

Park and ride (pages 58–59)

1 **Photo 1 (left):** a tram. A tram is a vehicle which carries passengers and travels along metal tracks in the street. **Note:** in contrast a trolleybus is a bus which is powered by overhead electric wires.

Photo 2 (centre): a maglev train. A maglev train uses magnetic force.

Photo 3 (right): a ferry. A ferry is a boat which takes passengers across a river or area of water.

2 A **captain** is in charge of a boat (or plane). A **chauffeur** is employed to drive a private or hired car. A **courier** delivers packages usually by van or bike. A **driver** drives a car, taxi, van, lorry (truck), train, bus, tram, trolleybus. A **motorist** drives a car. A **pilot** operates a plane or spaceship. A **pedestrian** walks.

4b **a)** reliable **b)** diversion **c)** convenient **d)** stuck **e)** Fuel prices **f)** maintenance **g)** transport

5a **A** park and ride **B** congestion charge **C** car share / carpool **D** toll road

Catch some zzz! (pages 60–61)

2a 1 catch up on sleep 2 sleep like a log 3 sleep in
4 not sleep a wink 5 get your beauty sleep
6 be in a deep sleep 7 lose sleep 8 be fast asleep

2b a) 3 sleep in b) 4 not sleep a wink c) 5 get your beauty
sleep d) 1 catch up on sleep e) 7 lose sleep f) 2 sleep
like a log / 6 be in a deep sleep / 8 be fast asleep

3b **relax:** calm down, chill out, switch off

worry: dwell on, stress out

worried: worked up

4a **A** 2 **B** 3 **C** 1

4b a) contacting b) unwind c) tense d) treat myself
e) concerns f) calming

A helping hand (pages 62–63)

1 a) got … across b) got on with c) got down to
d) get into e) get to f) got along with

2a 1 A 2 A 3 C 4 B 5 C

3a **not get anywhere:** not make any progress; **get hold
of:** make contact with; **get someone's attention:** make
someone notice you; **not get over:** be very surprised or
shocked by something

3b a) get along with / get on with b) get to c) get hold of
d) get over e) attention f) get on with / get down to
g) get across h) getting anywhere

Home is where the heart is (pages 64–65)

1a 1 attic / loft 2 garden / yard **Note:** *garden* (UK) and
yard (USA) both describe outdoor spaces belonging to a
house – these may well have a lawn. It is also possible to
use *yard* in British English to describe a small paved area
without grass and surrounded by walls, which some
houses in the UK have.
3 terrace / patio 4 roof garden 5 utility room
6 garage 7 basement / cellar **Note:** *basement* and
cellar are both used for a room under a building;
basement is also used to refer to an area or floor below
ground level, e.g. *basement flat*.

1b solar panels, central heating, micro wind turbine, sound
system

1c a) You can sit on a bench or a stool. You can put things
in a cupboard or shed. You can put things on a hook or a
counter. (You could also put things on a bench or stool.)

b) **Suggested answers**

bench: in a kitchen or porch; **counter:** in a kitchen;
cupboard: in a kitchen or garage; **hook:** in a bedroom,
bathroom, porch or hall; **shed:** in a garden or yard;
stool: in a kitchen, living room or bedroom

3a a) feel b) make c) place d) heart e) home

4 a) three-storey **Note:** We say either *a three-storey
building or a building with three floors* (but not *a three
floor building*) b) escalators (lifts go up and down) c)
corridor d) residential e) construction f) campus g)
setting h) properties

5 **Suggested answers**

comfortable: furniture, clothing, situations (e.g. *I
feel comfortable talking in class*.); **contemporary:**
music, fashion, decor, literature, art; **cosy:** clothing,
a café; **luxurious:** a car, decor, fabrics; **spacious:** a
car, an office; **stylish:** a person, decor, a restaurant;
traditional: beliefs, music, dance, customs, methods
(e.g. farming)

Festival fun (pages 66–67)

1a The photo shows Up Helly Aa. Harbin International Snow
and Ice festival is a winter festival and competition where
sculptures are made. Holi celebrates the arrival of Spring
and is also a time for forgiving and forgetting. Up Helly Aa
celebrates the end of the Christian festival of Christmas.

2 a) decorating b) performed c) dress up in / put on
d) marks / celebrates e) gather f) took place

4a 1 is held 2 celebration 3 origin 4 displays 5
traditional dress 6 sculptures 7 custom 8 highlight

Fair trade (pages 68–69)

2b 1 Liv 2 Liv 3 Adrian 4 Maya 5 Maya 6 Liv

2c a) organic (adj) b) exploit (v) c) chain (n)
d) vegan (n) e) brand (n) f) produce (n) g) benefits (n)
h) packaging (n)

4 browse (v) / look around (v)
in stock (phr) / available (adj)
bring out (v) / launch (v)
purchase (v) / buy (v)
cheap (adj) / inexpensive (adj)
bargain (v) / negotiate (v)

Author: Helen Chilton

Publisher: Gordon Knowles

Senior Development Editor: Fiona Davis

Designer: Tim Stephens

Cover Design: Eddie Rego

Picture Research: Suzanne Williams/Pictureresearch.co.uk

The publishers are grateful for permission to reproduce and adapt the following copyright materials:

Pages 8–9: Adapted from "What a Waste!" Published in SCHOLASTIC SCIENCE WORLD. November 20, 2017. Copyright © 2017 by Scholastic Inc. Reprinted by permission.

Pages 18–19: Adapted from "Fighting Drought with Oranges" Published in SCHOLASTIC SCIENCE WORLD. October 9, 2017. Copyright © 2017 by Scholastic Inc. Reprinted by permission.

Pages 20–21: Adapted from "Should Plastic Bags be Banned?" "Yes" by Lance Rothchild; "No" by Vedika Jawa. Published in SCHOLASTIC CHOICES, January 2018. Copyright © 2018 by Scholastic Inc. Reprinted by permission.

Pages 22–23: Adapted from "How Pokemon GO Conquered the World". Published in SCHOLASTIC ACTION, December 2016 – January 2017. Copyright © 2016 by Scholastic Inc. Reprinted by permission

Page 25: Adapted from "Should Teens Do Extreme Sports?" Published in SCHOLASTIC CHOICES, October 2016. Copyright © 2016 by Scholastic Inc. Reprinted by permission..

Pages 30–31: Adapted from "How Well Do you Know … You?" by Andrea Bartz. Published in SCHOLASTIC CHOICES, October 2017. Copyright © 2017 by Scholastic Inc. Reprinted by permission.

Pages 36–37: Adapted from "Are you Following the Herd?" by Holly Corbett. Published in SCHOLASTIC CHOICES, May 2017. Copyright © 2017 by Scholastic Inc. Reprinted by permission.

Page 42: Adapted from "How Healthy Are You … Really?" by Margarita Bertsos. Published in SCHOLASTIC CHOICES, September 2016. Copyright © 2016 by Scholastic Inc. Reprinted by permission.

Page 45: Adapted from "10 Truth Bombs About 'Perfect' Fitness Selfies" by Virginia Dole Smith. Published in SCHOLASTIC CHOICES, January 2018. Copyright © 2018 by Scholastic Inc. Reprinted by permission.

Pages 52–53: Adapted from "How do you say 'Yum' Around the World?" Published in SCHOLASTIC CHOICES, October 2017. Copyright © 2017 by Scholastic Inc. Reprinted by permission.

Pages 60–61: Adapted from "Generation Zzzzzzzz". Published in SCHOLASTIC CHOICES, September 2017. Copyright © 2017 by Scholastic Inc. Reprinted by permission.

Picture credits:
t = top, b = bottom, l = left, r = right, c = centre
Alamy Stock Photo: pp 57 (ccl/Justin Kase ztwoz), (br/Martin Bond), 58 (tc/Panther Media GmbH);
Getty Images: p 18 (l/Deon Raath/Foto24/ Gallo Images);
iStockphoto: pp 6 (l/shironosov), (c/skynesher), (r/skynesher), 8 (r/choice76), 10 (l/Antagain), (cl/gallinagomedia), (cr/GlobalP), (r/Lipowski), 12 (c/Ig0rZh), (r/Lysogor), 14 (c/PeopleImages), (r/SensorSpot), 16 (cr/philipimage), 18 (r/cinoby), 26 (tl/praetorianphoto), (bl/alvarez), 27 (b/franckreporter), 28 (RoterPanther), 30 (l/tanukiphoto), (cl/pixonaut), (cr/edwindejongh), (r/Labbas2), 32 (tl/milindri), (tcl/MediaProduction), (tcr/WendyOlsenPhotography), (b/deimagine), 33 (bo1982), 34 (tr/valentinrussanov), (cl/somchaij), (cr/Joel Carillet), (bl/vgajic), (br/Ceneri), 38 (c/urbanglimpses), (b/Dar07), 40 (tr/ebstock), (cr/AntonioDiaz), 42 (l/visualspace), 51 (tr/Shantell), (br/acidgrey), (1/starfish123), (2/bluestocking), (3/dulezidar), (4/Barcin), (5/Floortje), (6/anna1311), (7/Suzifoo), 54 (tr/sturti), (cr/mihailomilovanovic), (bl/monkeybusinessimages), 55 (l/sturti), (r/IPGGutenbergUKLtd), 57 (cl/MagMos), 58 (bl/Tassii), (br/annebaek), 60 (br/Linda Raymond), 62 (Steve Debenport), 64 (elenabs), 66 (HelenL100), 68 (cl/Ismailciydem), (cr/lubilub), (bl/Tassii);
Shutterstock: pp 8 (l/Kunertus), (c/amophotoau), 11 (Ardely), 12 (l/Sergey Nivens), 14 (l/Ranta Images), 16 (l/stockphotoworld), (cl/Solis Images), (r/PrinceOfLove), 22 (Stoyan Yotov), 24 (t/lightpoet), (b/Ammit Jack), 26 (tc/Aisyaqilumaranas), (tr/Ikonoklast Fotografie), (br/DW labs Incorporated), 27 (t/pixelheadphoto digitalskillet), 32 (tr/Sergey Zaykov), 36 (VGstockstudio), 38 (t/Yauhen Stayanovich), 39 (l/Djomas), (r/Dusan Petkovic), 40 (cl/silverkblackstock), (b/Olena Yakobchuk), 42 (r/Stockfotografie), 44 (M.Stasy), 47 (Happy Stock Photo), 48 (Tithi Luadthong), 49 (Lario Tus), 50 (l/FashionStock.com), (cl/GaudiLab), (cr/ivankislitsin), (r/Kaponia Aliaksei), 51 (tl/James Steidl), (bl/Ljupco Smokovski), 52 (b/Blend Images), 53 (l/Rachata Teyparsit), (r/imagedb.com), 54 (br/hedgehog94), 56 (zebrik), 57 (ccr/Photographee.eu), (cr/brizmaker), (bl/Artazum), 58 (tl/tateyama), (tr/cdrin), 60 (tr/Marcos Mesa Sam Wordley), (bl/ESB Essentials), (bc/Ranta Images), 65 (johavel), 67 (r/Billion Photos), (l/Gabor Kovacs Photography), 68 (tr/Rawpixel.com);
Courtesy of MEDASSET: p 20.